How to Create Compelling Mixes

How to Create Compelling Mixes

Craig Anderton

Hal Leonard Books
An Imprint of Hal Leonard LLC

Published in 2019 by Hal Leonard Books
An Imprint of Hal Leonard LLC
7777 West Bluemound Road
Milwaukee, WI 53213

Trade Book Division Editorial Offices
33 Plymouth St., Montclair, NJ 07042

The following photo is provided courtesy of Primeacoustic: Figure 2.4.

The following photo is provided courtesy of Sweetwater.com: Figure 9.6.

Printed in the United States of America

Book design by NextPoint Training, Inc.

Library of Congress Cataloging-in-Publication Data

Names: Anderton, Craig, author.
Title: How to create compelling mixes / Craig Anderton.
Description: Montclair, NJ : Hal Leonard Books, 2019. | Series: Musician's
  guide to home recording
Identifiers: LCCN 2018058309 | ISBN 9781540024886
Subjects: LCSH: Sound recordings--Production and direction. | Popular
  music--Production and direction.
Classification: LCC ML3790 .A642 2019 | DDC 781.49--dc23
LC record available at https://lccn.loc.gov/2018058309

www.halleonardbooks.com

Contents

Acknowledgments xiii

Introduction. About This Book 1

    Considerations of Modern Mixing 1

    Tips and References 2

Chapter 1. Mixing Philosophies 3

    Are You a Musician, Producer, or Engineer? 3

    Right Brain vs. Left Brain 4

        How to Stay in Right-Brain Mode 4

    The Importance of "Feel" 5

    The Importance of the Arrangement 5

        Make Sure *Every* Part Serves the Song 6

        Build to the Moments of Impact 6

        The Mute Button's Importance 6

        You Have *Ten Seconds* to Grab Someone's Attention 6

        Think About Your Audience 7

    What's Your Intended Result? 7

    Key Takeaways 8

Chapter 2. Technical Basics 9

    Hearing and Frequency Response 9

        The Problem with Ears 10

        Optimum Mixing Levels 11

    Monitoring and Acoustics 12

        The Room 12

        Near-Field Monitors 15

        Anatomy of the Near-Field Monitor 16

        Rear-Panel Controls 17

        What's the Best Monitor? 19

        Learning Your Speaker and Room 19

    Test Your Mix on Multiple Playback Systems 20

    Key Takeaways 21

Chapter 3. Basics of Mixing with Computers..**23**

    Mixer Architecture 23

        Mono vs. Stereo Tracks..24

        Bus Basics..24

        Channel Strips...25

        About Grouping..27

    Unique Aspects of Mixing with Digital Audio..30

        The Two Kinds of Resolution..30

        The Two Types of Audio...30

        Setting Levels with Digital Mixers 33

        The Best Sample Rate for Recording and Mixing..34

    Key Takeaways..37

Chapter 4. How to Use Plug-Ins **39**

    Plug-In Technologies 39

    Plug-In Formats...40

        32-Bit vs. 64-Bit Plug-Ins 41

        Plug-In Wrappers...41

    Stereo vs. Mono Plug-Ins 41

    Effects Plug-Ins Are Always "Re-Amping" 42

    The Four Places to Insert Effects 42

        Track (Channel) Insert Effects..42

        Clip (Event) Effects..43

        Send Effects..44

        Master Effects...47

    Using Virtual Instrument Plug-Ins 48

        Instruments with Multiple Outputs..48

        ReWire and Mixing 49

    Using Hardware Effects when Mixing...53

        Limitations of External Hardware...53

        Setting Up for External Hardware 54

    Key Takeaways..56

Chapter 5. Mixing and MIDI **57**

    Mixing's Most Important MIDI Data 57

    Virtual Instruments and CPU Issues 58

Enhancing MIDI Drum Parts in the Mix 58
   Shift Pitch 58
   Change the Sample Start Point 59
   Filter Modulation 60
   Hi-Hat Amplitude Envelope Decay Modulation 60
   Mute Groups 60
Enhancing Synth Parts in the Mix 61
   Layering Techniques 61
   Taming Peaks 62
   Synth/Sampler Parameter Automation Applications 63
Humanizing Sequences 66
How Timing Shifts Produce "Feel" 66
   Track Timing Tricks 67
   How to Shift Individual Notes 68
   Quantization Options 69
Tempo Track Timing Tweaks 72
   Tempo and Mixing 73
   Inserting "Time Traps" 73
Proofing MIDI Sequences 74
Key Takeaways 75

Chapter 6. Preparing for the Mix 77
Before You Mix 78
Mental Preparation, Organization, and Setup 78
Review the Tracks 79
   Organize Your Mixer Space 79
   Put on Headphones and Listen for Glitches 80
Render Soft Synths as Audio Tracks 80
Set Up a Relative Level Balance Among the Tracks 80
Key Takeaways 81

Chapter 7. Adjusting Equalization 83
Overview 83
Equalizer Responses 84
Main EQ Parameters 87
Dynamic Equalization 89
Spectrum Analysis 90

Linear-Phase Equalization..91

    Linear-Phase Basics 91

    Limitations 92

    Minimizing Latency 93

Mid-Side Processing with Equalization..93

The Pros—and Pitfalls—of Presets 94

EQ Applications 95

    Solve Problems 96

    Emphasize Instruments 101

    Create New Sonic Personalities...101

Additional Equalization Tips 102

Key Takeaways...103

Chapter 8. Adding Dynamics Processing 105

Manual Gain-Riding..106

Level-Riding Plug-Ins 106

Normalization..107

Limiter 107

    Limiter Parameters and Controls 108

    How to Adjust the Parameters 109

Compressor 110

    Compressor Parameters..111

    How to Adjust the Parameters 113

    Parameter Adjustment Tips 114

    Multiband Compressor..115

Loudness Maximizer..116

Expander..117

Transient Shaper..118

Noise Gate 119

    Noise Gate Parameters...120

Sidechaining 122

Should Compression Go Before or After EQ?...............................123

Key Takeaways...124

Chapter 9. Adding Other Effects 125

Console Emulation 125

    Console Emulation Basics...126

    Inserting Console Emulation Plug-Ins 127

Console Channel Strips 128

Can You *Really* Hear a Difference? 129

Tape Emulation 129

Where to Insert Tape Emulation Plug-Ins 131

Distortion 131

Saturation 131

Where to Insert EQ with Distortion 135

Delay 136

Delay Parameters 136

Other Delay Features 137

Creating Wider-than-Life Sounds with Delay 139

Using Delay to Create Long, Trailing Echoes 140

Stereo Image Enhancers 140

Modulation Effects (Chorus, Flanger, etc.) 141

Chorus and Flanger Parameters 142

Modulation Effects Tips 143

Where to Insert Modulation Effects 143

Auto-Pan and Tremolo 144

De-Esser 144

Multieffects Plug-Ins 145

Pitch Correction 146

How Pitch Correction Works 147

Applying Pitch Correction 147

Other Pitch Correction Applications 147

Where to Insert Pitch Correction 149

Pitch Transposer 149

Exciter 150

Restoration Plug-Ins 151

Multiband Processing 151

Step 1: Create Parallel Signal Chains (Splits) 152

Step 2: Create Frequency Bands 154

Step 3: Start Processing 156

Key Takeaways 157

Chapter 10. Creating a Stereo Soundstage **159**

Panning Basics 159

How Panning Differs for Stereo and Mono Tracks 160

Panning and MIDI 161

Panning Tips 161

Binaural Panning 162

The Audio Architect: Building Your Acoustical Space 163

About Reverb 164

The Different Reverb Types 164

One Reverb or Many? 165

Supplementing Reverb with a Real Acoustic Space 166

Reverb Parameters and Controls 167

Create Virtual Room Mics with Delay 170

The Setup 170

Editing Parameters Other than Delay Times 171

Additional Short Delay Tips 171

Plan Ahead with Reverb and Panning 172

Key Takeaways 172

Chapter 11. Using Mix Automation **173**

What You Can Automate 173

Automation Basics 174

Automation Methods 175

Method 1: Record On-Screen Control Motion 175

Method 2: Draw/Edit Envelopes 176

Method 3: Recording Automation Moves from External Control Hardware 177

Method 4: Snapshot Automation 178

Automating Plug-Ins 178

Fixed Controller Automation 179

MIDI Learn 179

Using Hardware Control Surfaces 180

Traditional Mixing 180

How to Choose a Control Surface 181

Adding a Control Surface to Your Setup 182

Automation Applications 183

Adding Expressiveness with Controllers 184

Aux Send Automation and Delays 184

Aux Sends and Reverb Splashes 185

Panning 185

Complementary Motion 185

Mutes and Solos 185

Mute vs. Change Level 185

Plug-In Automation Applications 186

    Better Chorusing and Flanging 186

    Creative Distortion Crunch 186

    Emphasizing with EQ 186

    Delay Feedback 187

    Sweeping the Parametric Wah 187

    Envelope-Based Tremolo 188

    Pseudo Sample-and-Hold Effects 188

Virtual Instrument Automation Applications 189

    Virtual Guitar Feedback 189

    Suboctave with Bass 189

    Synthesizer Pads 189

    Fun with Ostinato and Arpeggiation 189

Key Takeaways 190

Chapter 12. Review and Export **191**

Mastering While Mixing—Pros and Cons 191

    Online and Automated Mastering Services 192

    Mastering While Mixing 193

    Prepping Files for a Mastering Engineer 193

Export Your Mixed File 194

    Main File Types 194

    Sample Rates and Bit Depth 195

    Bouncing Mixes Inside the Project 196

Check Your Mix Over Different Systems 197

Key Takeaways 198

Appendix. Mixing with Noise **199**

Why Mixing Can Be Challenging 199

The Backstory Behind Using Noise 199

Mixing with Noise 200

    Getting Started with Noise Injection 200

    Setting Levels with Noise 200

    Noise Zones 201

Summary 201

Acknowledgments

A series like this is never the work of one person, but rather a collection of the experiences obtained over the years from too many people to acknowledge here. Yet some deserve a special mention.

Dan Earley, my editor at Music Sales, who was the first person to say, "You know what would be cool? A series of books on recording, like those Time Life libraries." Well Dan, better late than never, right?

Sir George Martin, who was kind enough to write the foreword to my 1977 book, *Home Recording for Musicians*. He asked for samples of my writing, and I thought that would be the end of it. Instead, he wrote an eloquent foreword that set a wonderful tone for the book. He truly was the consummate gentleman everyone says he was.

The team at Hal Leonard—especially John Cerullo, who green-lighted this series and brought in Frank D. Cook to serve as the editor for these books.

My father, who taught me that it didn't matter if I was a dreadful writer as long as I could edit my words into something readable—and who also showed me what it meant to love music.

My mother, who with my father was unfailingly supportive when I wanted to do things like drop out of college, join a rock band, go on tour, and never look back!

My brother, who understood music on a very deep level and died too young.

And of course, the many *(many)* engineers and producers who let me look over their shoulders and absorb knowledge like a sponge over the past five decades. My hope is that this series will help pass their collective wisdom on to another generation.

Introduction

About This Book

Welcome to the book series Musician's Guide to Home Recording. This series of short publications was written to address the needs of musicians and recording enthusiasts who are interested in creating self-produced songs or doing audio production work for others.

Rather than trying to cover all aspects of recording in a single sprawling volume, each title in the series concisely and accessibly addresses a particular subject. You can select individual titles to hone in on certain skills or proceed through the entire series; this kind of approach lets you develop a comprehensive knowledge at your own pace.

This book, *How to Create Compelling Mixes*, covers not just the technology of mixing, but also the artistic philosophy.

Considerations of Modern Mixing

Perhaps no other area of recording has been affected by technology as much as mixing. What used to require expensive multitrack recorders, huge mixing consoles, and a substantial investment in outboard gear—like musical instruments and signal processors—now fits in a computer… at a fraction of the cost.

What hasn't changed is that you still have to learn about mixing technology and techniques. It doesn't matter if a mixing console or synthesized instrument is represented by pixels on a computer screen or controls on a piece of hardware, creating a great mix is a complex and sometimes daunting process. It's as if you'd walked into a million-dollar studio a few decades ago and the owner said, "Good news. I'll charge you only a dollar an hour for studio time; however, there's no engineer. Good luck!" and handed you the keys.

This book is all about the many facets of the mixing process in our computer–based world. No one will claim that learning how to mix is easy, but the goal of this book is to make it less difficult—and to remind you that the whole purpose of making music is to enjoy yourself, give your listeners an emotional experience, be creative, and maybe even discover a little bit more about who you are.

Ready? Let's start mixing.

Tips and References

This book includes various tips, definitions, cross-references, and other supplemental nuggets throughout its pages. These are denoted with the following icons and formatting.

 Tips and side notes provide helpful hints and suggestions, background information, or additional details on a concept or topic.

 Definitions provide explanations of technical terms, industry jargon, or abbreviations.

 Cross-References alert you to another section, book, or online resource that provides additional information on the current topic.

 Warnings caution you against conditions that may have adverse effects or unexpected results.

Chapter 1

Mixing Philosophies

Mixing is the process of taking the tracks you recorded and crafting them into a cohesive listening experience. This involves adjusting the levels, tonal balance, and stereo or surround placement, and adding appropriate signal processing until everything sounds great. While that may seem straightforward, completing a mix requires a huge number of value judgments—which instrument should get the focus at any given moment, should some unneeded parts be muted or erased, do you want a raw or highly produced sound, and perhaps most importantly, who is your target audience, and what do *they* want to hear? Your mix's success depends on your ability to answer and resolve these questions.

Mixing is a combination of art—you have to judge what's most *musical*—and science, where you need to know the processes, technologies, and settings that will produce the sounds you want to hear. In a way, mixing is like a combination lock: once all the tumblers are in place, the lock will open.

Are You a Musician, Producer, or Engineer?

In professional studios, the musician is typically part of a team that includes at least a producer and an engineer. In a home studio environment, you may need to perform all three roles. It's not easy to step out of the musician mindset and learn to be objective about your playing, songwriting, and engineering. However, if you do, your music will benefit greatly. Here's each participant's role:

♦ The **producer** oversees the process, approves the arrangement, gauges the overall emotional impact, and makes artistic judgments about what does and does not work. A producer sees each aspect of the mixing process as part of a whole, and each track as a contributor to the final composition. If you know where you're going, it's a lot easier to get there.

♦ The **musician** participates in the mix by making sure the production remains true to the original artistic vision.

♦ The **engineer** is the person who fulfills the producer's needs with technological solutions. If the producer wants a "bigger" drum sound, the engineer tweaks the equipment to produce the desired effect. Engineers don't worry about whether the musicians could have given a better performance; they work with what's available.

Before setting out to mix a project, it helps to become familiar with these roles. Applying their differing outlooks to your music will allow you to obtain a balanced perspective. Mixing isn't just about blending tracks, but producing a musical experience from blending those tracks.

It's equally important not to overproduce. Sometimes tracks are best left unprocessed. Other times you may need to delete parts to create space for more important parts. Be careful not to fall in love with the elements that make up a particular piece of music; keep your focus on what makes the strongest final result. Every part should support the music. Although a dazzling guitar lick might be impressive, it might also be a distraction at a particular moment in a song.

Right Brain vs. Left Brain

Although an oversimplification, the human brain is a dual-processing system. The left hemisphere handles more analytical tasks, while the right hemisphere is more involved with creative tasks and emotional responses. This can affect mixing because it's difficult to switch between the two hemispheres. For example, suppose you're in a creative mode and your mix is progressing well. If a technical glitch occurs, you have to switch over to analytical mode and begin troubleshooting. When you return to the mix, you may find the magic is gone—the glitch stuck you in left-brain mode.

In a conventional studio situation, the engineer handles the left-brain tasks, the artist can stay in right-brain mode, and the producer works to integrate the two. Performing all these functions yourself is a major challenge, but it is not an insurmountable one.

How to Stay in Right-Brain Mode

One of the best ways to stay in right-brain mode is to make left-brain activities second nature so you don't have to think about them. Here are some tips:

♦ **Learn keyboard shortcuts.** It's less effort to hit a couple of keys than to locate an area on the screen, move your mouse to it, go down a menu, select an item, etc. You may also be able to trigger functions from a keyboard or other controller, like assigning controls on a MIDI keyboard to your software's transport functions—play, rewind, etc.

♦ **Create macros.** Some programs can create *macros*, which combine strings of keyboard commands into a single command. Third-party programs for creating macros include AutoHotkey for Windows and Keyboard Maestro for Mac.

♦ **Use window layouts.** Layouts, also called screensets, organize windows for specific tasks (e.g., mixing, overdubbing, MIDI editing, and the like) so you needn't keep opening and closing windows or dragging them around. Calling up these layouts with keyboard shortcuts saves even more time.

♦ **Make good use of color.** The brain decodes colors and images more easily than words. For example, I color vocal tracks green, guitar tracks blue, etc. so they're easy to pick out when working with a large number of tracks. Track icons with pictures of instruments initially struck me as cartoonish, but it's easier to locate an instrument by seeing a picture than reading a label.

The Importance of "Feel"

Some older recordings created under technically primitive conditions still have a great "feel" that makes you want to listen to them over and over again. Although the musicians' performances accounted for a lot of that feel, the mix could also be a performance factor—especially when the mix involved a large console with different people "playing" different faders. That principle remains true today.

Some producers prioritize feel and aren't concerned about minor technical errors or musical glitches. Others seek perfection by recording parts dozens of times or splicing together bits from multiple takes. Both approaches are valid, but it's best to avoid tilting too much in one direction. Some musicians are so self-critical they never finish a mix. Try to avoid this, but don't be so forgiving that you let issues slip through you'll regret later. One of the great aspects of working with producers is their ability to pinpoint what can be improved in your music. Always ask yourself what can make the mix better, but realize that getting too obsessed with detail can take the life out of a mix. It's a fine line.

Technology can help thanks to *automation* (see Chapter 11), which stores your mixing moves and makes it possible to save different mixes. The initial mixes may have an energy later mixes lack, so remember to save often and work in stages. You may decide to combine different parts from different mixes—the first verse from one mix, the chorus from another, and so on. Import the mixes into your program, cut and paste the appropriate sections, then export the final result.

It's even possible during the mixing process to give parts more feel.

Details on adding feel during a mix are provided in Chapter 5.

The Importance of the Arrangement

Mixing is your last chance to alter the arrangement. The ability of one person to write, play, produce, record, master, and even duplicate music is a fairly recent development; traditionally, music has been a collaborative process. Getting input from a trusted associate who can give honest, objective feedback is invaluable. If that's not possible, you need to figure out how to provide some of the objectivity and detachment a producer provides. It's not easy, but here are some recommendations on how to look at your arrangement.

Make Sure *Every* Part Serves the Song

You may be really proud of a particular riff, but does it serve the song? The main lesson I learned from my studio musician years is that with vocal-based music, everything exists to help the singer tell the story. Your licks are there only to make the lead vocal more effective.

Writing a part without considering the song's context can be a problem. I once came up with a lyrical, melodic bass part for a verse while waiting for the engineer to dial in a snare drum sound. I thought it was a really good part. Unfortunately, when mixed with the vocal, it was distracting. I ended up playing an ultra-simple part that anyone could play—but the simpler version made a far greater contribution to the tune.

Build to the Moments of Impact

Sometimes vocalists double their vocals to create a "bigger" sound. However, that practice can reduce the vocal's intimacy if layering the two vocals obscures some vocal nuances. In a case like this, try muting the doubled part until it's really needed: to add extra emphasis to a hook when it reappears or for a big chorus.

As another example, try dropping instruments out so they have more impact when they return. DJs excel at this—they'll take the kick drum and bass out for a while, and then when those instruments return, the drama is palpable. If the bass is absent during the intro, it will have more impact when it finally enters. I also like to mute drums in the middle of a song for a few measures, and let the vocals and other instruments carry the tune for a while. This adds an element of tension that's released when the drums return.

The Mute Button's Importance

For me, the console's most important button is the channel mute button. When mixing, I use it to find out whether a part is essential or not. Taking out a part makes what remains more important and provides contrast (which helps hold the listener's attention) as parts weave in and out of the arrangement.

Fewer parts also simplify the mixing process. If you have only two tracks in a song, like a singer and rhythm guitar, there's not much to mix. But when you have a zillion tracks, trying to find the right balance becomes far more difficult. Fewer tracks help a song "mix itself."

The mixing process is your last chance to be uncompromisingly honest. If something doesn't work quite right, get rid of it—regardless of how clever it is or how good it sounds on its own.

You Have *Ten Seconds* to Grab Someone's Attention

A song's intro will make or break your mix because you have to hook the listener immediately. This was even true decades ago, when radio station DJs would go through records by playing the first ten seconds. If something didn't grab them... "Next!"

Here's a test for intros. Picture an office party filled with a variety of people, from the new mailroom guy to upper management. They're all a bit tipsy and chatting away while some streaming service (whose quality isn't great) provides background music. Now imagine that your song starts playing.

How do the people react? Is there something in the first few seconds to grab their attention and keep it? Do they stop talking and listen? Do they listen for the first few bars, then go back to conversing? Do they ignore it entirely? Think of your music in the context of a *playlist*. It has to be able to segue from anything to anything, appeal to short attention spans, and be different. Also, remember a listener's first exposure may be on the Internet—where someone else's music is only a click away.

Think About Your Audience

Songs were once honed on the road, and the goal of recording was to capture that magic in the studio. Now songs are more often created in the studio and recreated on the road. As you mix a tune, always imagine an audience is listening. It will influence how the song develops.

One musician I know borrows his daughter's dolls and stuffed animals upon starting a mix. He sets them up so they're staring at him. It's like the initial audience environment at a bar, he claims—expressionless and bored—which reminds him to think about what would get an audience to react in some way. A mix can't just *play* your song: it has to *sell* your song.

What's Your Intended Result?

All this advice assumes that you *want* to connect with an audience. But is that important to you? Although it's great to communicate through the language of music, creating music can also be about self-discovery. Even if I were told no one would ever hear my songs, I'd still make music because music itself is magical.

I believe there are two main ways to be successful. One is to be totally true to yourself, and hope that the music you make strikes a chord in others. This creates the brightest stars with the longest careers because what they're doing comes naturally—they don't have to fake it. If the music you make doesn't "fit" with a mass audience, at least your friends will probably enjoy it because they know who you are already.

The other option is to study past hits carefully. Learn how they were arranged, pick lyrical subjects with wide appeal, and create mixes designed to appeal to specific audiences. That's fine, and it can lead to a comfortable, well-paying career. But it's not effortless; it still requires a strong creative spark, and for you you to be brutally honest about whether a piece of music has potential for mass appeal (spoiler alert: most of the time, the answer is "no").

Perhaps combining the two approaches yields the best results. Let the artist in you create, then let the hard-nosed, objective part of you create the mix. While this section has concentrated on what it takes to become more objective, I don't want to trivialize the creative factor. As in so many aspects of life, sometimes a synthesis of opposites creates the best results. Go ahead, love your music—but don't be *in love* with it if you want to remain objective.

Okay, enough opinions… let's get technical.

Key Takeaways

♦ If you work by yourself, you're not just the artist, but also the engineer and producer. These are very different skills.

♦ Make repetitive tasks second nature so that you can concentrate on being creative.

♦ Be careful not to prioritize perfection over feel.

♦ Mixing is your last chance to change the arrangement. Make sure every part serves the song.

♦ Mute tracks to determine whether they're necessary or not. Less can indeed be more.

♦ The beginning is crucial—you have ten seconds to grab someone's attention.

♦ Think about your music's intended result, and work toward making it happen.

Chapter 2

Technical Basics

The more you know the technology involved in mixing, the more easily you can take advantage of it. However, always remember that the most important—and technically complex—piece of gear used in mixing is the human ear. Let's start there.

Hearing and Frequency Response

Mixing's goal is to produce a balanced, even sound with a full, satisfying bass, a well-defined midrange, and sparkly (not screechy) highs. Equalization, which alters *frequency response*, helps make this possible.

Frequency response defines how a system records or reproduces the audible frequencies from 20 Hz to 20,000 Hz. On a frequency response graph that shows levels at different frequencies, the Y-axis (vertical) shows level, and the X-axis (horizontal) indicates frequency (Fig. 2.1).

 The abbreviation Hz is short for hertz, which measures the number of cycles per second in a wave; 1 kHz or kilohertz equals 1,000 Hz.

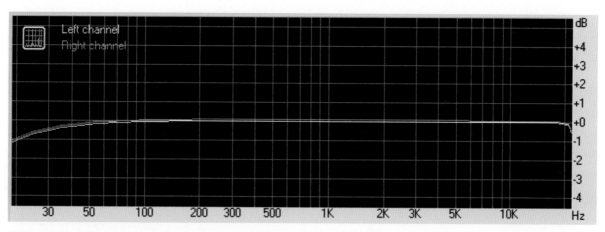

Figure 2.1 This graph shows the frequency response for an audio interface. The bass response drops off somewhat in the bass frequencies.

The audible range is further divided into bands. There's no official definition of the frequencies that each band covers, but the following is a general representation:

◆ Bass: Lowest frequencies, typically below 200 Hz.

◆ Lower midrange: 200 to 500 Hz.

◆ Midrange: 500 Hz to 2.5 kHz.

◆ Upper midrange: 2.5 kHz to 5 kHz.

◆ Treble: 5 kHz and higher.

While these guidelines are approximate, they are still useful. For example, bass guitar and kick drum occupy the bass range. Vocals are in the midrange and lower midrange. Percussion instruments like tambourine have lots of energy in the treble region.

Note that although electronic devices can have a flat frequency response, no mechanical device does. A speaker's response falls off at high and low frequencies. Guitar pickup response falls off at high frequencies, which is why guitar amps often boost the upper midrange. Pothing's nerfect.

The Problem with Ears

Your ears' limitations become more pronounced if you abuse your hearing (e.g., listen to loud music for prolonged periods of time, do deep sea diving, drink a lot of alcohol, etc.). Even flying can affect your ears' high frequency response. I'll wait at least 24 hours after flying before mixing or mastering; the few times I've disregarded that rule, mixes that seemed fine played back too bright the next day. And no matter how well you take care of your hearing, age will take its toll.

But even healthy, young ears aren't perfect. The ear has a midrange peak and does not respond as well to low and high frequencies, particularly at lower volumes. The response comes closest to flat response at relatively high levels.

The Fletcher-Munson curve (Fig. 2.2) illustrates this phenomenon. This illustration depicts a set of equal-loudness contours for the human ear. These contours show the sound levels required across the frequency spectrum for our ear to perceive an equal loudness across those frequencies.

At low listening levels, the low and high frequency ranges require a substantial boost to be heard at equal volume to the midrange frequencies. At higher listening levels, the contours start to flatten out, meaning the lows and highs begin to sound more prominent without requiring the same boost.

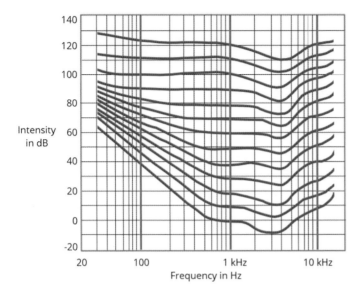

Figure 2.2 The Fletcher-Munson curve shows the listening levels required to produce an equal perceived volume at different frequencies. At low levels, low frequencies need to be boosted substantially to be perceived as having a volume equal to midrange frequencies.

It's crucial to care for your hearing. In my touring days, when I'd often play 200 days out of the year, I would pack cotton in my ears. While not as effective as present-day earplugs, I'm sure it helped preserve my hearing.

Today, I often carry the cylindrical foam earplugs available at sporting good stores and wear them while walking city streets, visiting at clubs, hammering or using power tools, or anytime my ears are going to get more abuse than normal conversational-level sound. I make my living with my ears, so taking care of them is a priority.

 Schedule an appointment with an audiologist at least once every year or two. Some hearing issues that lead to deafness can be prevented if caught in time.

Optimum Mixing Levels

Loud mixes may be exciting, but loud, extended mixing sessions are tough on the ears. Mixing at low levels keeps your ears "fresher" and minimizes ear fatigue; you'll also be able to discriminate better among subtle level variations. However, as mentioned, your ears' response will change at different levels. Although I start a mix at low levels, the volume increases over time to a consistent, comfortable level—one where I can listen for hours on end, with zero listening fatigue. That becomes the benchmark level.

After getting a good mix, I then check the mix again at low levels, and finally crank it for a "let's turn this sucker up" reality test. If at loud levels the mix sounds just a little too bright and boomy, and if at low levels it sounds just a bit bass- and treble-light, that's about right. When a mix is satisfactory at all levels, it will "translate" well over different playback systems. Of course, that assumes there aren't problems with your listening environment, so let's cover that next.

Monitoring and Acoustics

It's almost impossible to do a good mix if your monitoring system isn't honest about the sounds you hear. If a mix sounds great on your system but falls apart when played elsewhere on good systems, something's wrong with your monitoring process. The problem could be the speakers, the room acoustics, your hearing, or a combination of these factors.

The Room

The room in which you monitor your work influences how you mix. For a real shocker, set up an audio level meter (several smartphone apps can do the job reasonably well, such as Decibel X for iOS and Android), sit with it in the middle of your room, run a sine wave test tone through the speakers, and watch the meter. Unless you have great monitors and an acoustically tuned room, that meter will fluctuate like a leaf in a windstorm. Monitor speakers don't have perfectly flat responses, but they look ruler-flat compared to the average untreated room.

You don't even need a level meter to conduct this test: Play a steady tone around 5 kHz or so, then move your head around. You'll hear obvious volume fluctuations. (If you can't hear the 5 kHz tone, you should consider switching careers!) These variations occur because as sound bounces off walls, the reflections become part of the overall sound. This creates signal cancellations and additions.

Another example of how acoustics affects sound occurs when you place a speaker against a wall, which seems to increase bass. This is because any sounds emanating from the rear of the speaker bounce off the wall. These reflections reinforce the main wave coming from the speaker's front.

Because the walls, floors, and ceilings all interact with your speakers, it's important to place the speakers symmetrically within a room. If (for example) one speaker is three feet from a wall and another is ten feet from a wall, any reflections will be wildly different and this will affect the response.

The subject of acoustical treatment deserves a book in itself, but here are some tips:

♦ **Avoid walls and corners.** Try not to place speakers right in front of a wall or in a corner.

♦ **Don't sit close to walls when mixing.** Avoid a listening position where your ears are less than three feet (one meter) from any wall. My recording setup with mixer, controller, and computer keyboard is arranged on tables within the front third of the room. This reduces reflection buildup of peak frequencies, and also frees up the wall space for a combination of shelves and acoustical treatment.

The "middle of the room" approach also makes it easier to deal with the cables running among the gear's rear panels.

♦ **Center your setup's left and right sides.** Place your left and right speakers an equal distance from their respective walls. This will produce balanced mid- and low-frequency response and preserve stereo imaging.

♦ **Keep the mixing area uncluttered.** Avoid large objects (such as lamps or decorations) near the studio monitor and listening position—sorry, the lava lamp has to go.

♦ **Use diffusion and absorption.** Diffusers and sound-absorbent material placed in a room help prevent reflections from entering the listening space. Carpeting minimizes reflections from hard floor surfaces.

♦ **Decouple (isolate) the speaker base from where it sits.** A thick piece of neoprene, or even a thick mouse pad, can help prevent vibrations from traveling into a stand or table that cause it to vibrate. I use Primacoustic's Recoil Stabilizers (Fig. 2.3).

Figure 2.3 The Primacoustic Recoil Stabilizer isolates a speaker from the surface on which it sits.

♦ **Minimize reflective surfaces between the speakers and your ears.** If the speakers are on a table along with gear like a mixer, place the speakers to the side of the mixer, and on small stands. You don't want waves reflecting off the table (or the mixer) and hitting your ears. Placing sound-absorbing material (like a thick rug) on top of the table can also help.

♦ **Place speaker fronts in front of monitor screens.** If your speakers are to the side of your computer monitors, make sure each speaker's front is in front of the monitor's screen. Being behind the screen or flush with it may affect the sound quality.

♦ **Reality test with headphones.** Test your mixes occasionally with high-quality, *circumaural* headphones. These will make room acoustics irrelevant. Sometimes you can even hear bass more accurately with headphones than with near-field monitors. However, avoid headphones designed for consumers, because they often "hype" the highs and lows to give deep bass and sizzling highs.

Circumaural headphones go over your ears, rather than sitting on top of them.

 Caution: It's easy to blast your ears with headphones and not know it. Watch those volume levels—and be *very* careful not to accidentally set up a feedback loop; a loud squeal could cause permanent hearing damage.

This is basic advice. Hiring a professional studio acoustics consultant to "tune" your room with bass traps and proper acoustic treatment could be the best investment you ever make in your music. Every room is different, so solutions differ (Fig. 2.4).

Figure 2.4 Acoustical treatment can improve room acoustics dramatically. Note the bass traps in the corners, and additional treatment on the ceiling.

Some people try to compensate for room anomalies by inserting a graphic equalizer between their mixer or audio interface and speakers, then tuning the equalization to adjust for frequency response variations. However if your position deviates at all from the *sweet spot* (the place at which the room acoustics were tuned), the frequency response will change. Also, heavily equalizing a poor-quality acoustical space simply gives you a heavily equalized, poor-quality acoustical space. Like noise reduction, which works best on signals without much noise, room tuning works best on rooms that don't have serious response problems.

Some tuning options are better than others. IK Multimedia's ARC2 room tuning system has worked well for me. It takes some time to set up (a flat response microphone to take measurements is also available), but the result is a better mixing environment. The ARC2 doesn't aim for one "perfect" spot at the expense of the rest of the room, but instead does an overall room adjustment. A plug-in compensates for the room acoustics while you mix (Fig. 2.5). Note that before exporting the final mix, you must bypass the plug-in.

Figure 2.5 The ARC2 system compensates for room acoustics issues. Part of the system is a plug-in that applies a correction curve so you can mix as if you were in a room with correct acoustics.

Near-Field Monitors

The traditional, big studios of the late 20th century had large monitors mounted at a considerable distance from the mixer (six to ten feet or so), with the front flush to the wall, and an acoustically treated control room to minimize response variations. The sweet spot was where the mixing engineer sat at the console. In smaller, project studios, near-field monitors have become the standard way to monitor (Fig. 2.6).

Figure 2.6 Typical near-field, two-way monitor speakers. Left to right: Focal Solo6 Be, KRK V-Series V6, and Yamaha HS7I. The V6 has a 6-inch woofer; the others have 6.5-inch woofers.

These relatively compact speakers sit around three to six feet from the mixer's ears, with the mixer's head and the speakers forming a triangle (Fig. 2.7).

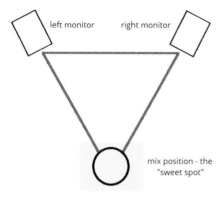

Figure 2.7 This top view of the mix position shows how the monitor speakers and the listener form an equilateral triangle.

Two-way monitors incorporate a tweeter (producing high frequencies) and a woofer (producing mid and low frequencies) in one enclosure. The full frequency range comes together at the *acoustic axis point,* which is between the tweeter and woofer. This should be at ear level in the listening position; you can angle the studio monitors if needed so the acoustic axis points at your ears.

Near-field monitors reduce (but do not eliminate) the impact of room acoustics, because the speakers' direct sound is louder than the reflections from the room surfaces. As a side benefit, near-field monitors needn't produce a lot of power because they're close to your ears.

However, room placement remains an issue. Being too close to the walls will boost the bass artificially. Although you can compensate somewhat using EQ (or possibly using controls on the speakers themselves, as discussed later), the build-up will differ at different frequencies. High frequencies are not as affected because they are more directional. If the speakers are freestanding and placed away from the wall, back reflections from the sound bouncing off the wall could cause cancellations and additions for the reasons mentioned earlier.

Placing speakers more than six feet away from the wall in a fairly large listening space works well, but not everyone has that much room. One option is to mount the speakers a bit away from the wall on the same table holding the mixer, and on stands so they're not sitting on the table itself. After creating a direct path from speaker to ear, pad the walls behind the speakers with as much sound-deadening material as possible.

Anatomy of the Near-Field Monitor

Near-field monitors are available in various sizes, at numerous price points. Most are two-way designs, with (typically) a 5-inch, 6-inch, or 8-inch woofer and smaller tweeter. A three-way design adds a separate midrange driver.

A three-way design is not necessarily better than a two-way design. A well-designed two-way system will be better than a poorly designed three-way system.

Although larger speaker sizes may be harder to fit in a small studio, the increase in low-frequency accuracy can be substantial. If your room is big enough to accommodate an 8-inch monitor, you may find it worth the extra expense for work with bass-heavy music like hip-hop and EDM.

There are two main monitor types, *active* and *passive.* Passive monitors consist of only the speakers and a *crossover* (the filter that splits the input to the low and high-frequency speakers). These monitors require an outboard amplifier. Active monitors incorporate the crossover and the amps needed to drive the speakers from a line-level signal. With good active monitors, the power amp and speaker have been tweaked into a smooth, efficient team. Issues such as speaker cable resistance become irrelevant, and protection can be built into the amp to prevent blowouts. Powered monitors are usually *bi-amped* (meaning they have a separate amp for the woofer and tweeter), which provides a cleaner sound and allows the manufacturer to optimize the crossover points and frequency response for the speakers being used.

If you hook up passive monitors to your own amps, make sure they have adequate headroom. Any clipping caused by the amp will generate lots of high-frequency harmonics. Sustained clipping can burn out tweeters.

Rear-Panel Controls

Because compensating for room acoustics can be a significant issue in today's studios, most manufacturers offer equalization options to compensate for acoustics-related problems. You'll see some or all of the following (Fig. 2.8), depending on the speaker model.

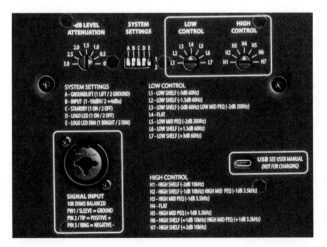

Figure 2.8 These controls on the rear panel of the KRK V-Series near-field monitor speakers offer multiple tone-shaping options.

Low-Shelf Control

Low-shelf cut options compensate for wall coupling where low-frequency sounds from the speaker's rear reinforce sounds coming from the speaker's front. Set the shelf for around 75 Hz for smaller models and 60 Hz for larger models, then apply a cut of between –1 and –3 dB—whatever gives the smoothest response.

On the other hand, boosting is useful when artists want to hear more bass than would be desirable for a mix or master. Some low-frequency boost at the speaker lets you mix with the correct amount of bass at the mixer, while giving artists what they want to hear.

Low-Mid Parametric Control

The Low-Mid control compensates for the lower midrange buildup that can occur if audio flows over a large console or other surface, which may muddy the sound. A typical setting is –2 dB at 200 Hz.

High-Mid Parametric Control

The ear is most sensitive in the 3 to 4 kHz range, and sadly, engineers who've mixed a lot at loud volumes may have hearing loss in that range. Boosting +1 dB at 3.5 kHz will help engineers mix these frequencies properly to compensate for hearing deficiencies. Applying a cut of around –1 dB at 3.5 kHz is a useful "Jedi mind trick" with artists who aren't confident about their voices. Reducing the perceived level at 3.5 kHz will make a voice sound less prominent at the speakers, but the actual mix will have the voice at the right level.

High-Frequency Control

High-frequency controls correct for mixing environments that are not bright enough or too bright, but can also be used for adjusting to taste. A high-shelf control is common, and if a speaker has only one high-frequency control, it will typically boost or cut around 2 dB at 10 kHz.

Input Sensitivity and Level Controls

The usual choices for sensitivity are –10 dB (for consumer and prosumer gear) and +4 dB (for pro-level, and often high-end, gear). However, note that input sensitivity is not a typical volume control: the amplifiers usually run at full gain, and then you adjust how "hard" you hit it with the input sensitivity control. As a result, you may obtain better results (more headroom, less noise) when running a system at +4 dB, assuming the device feeding the speaker can generate enough level.

A Caution about Rear Panel EQ Settings

It takes a while for the ear to acclimate to EQ and level changes. It's always best to start off with flat settings, and get to know your speakers and your room. Listen to music with which you are familiar, and preferably, have heard over quality monitors in a studio with good acoustics so you have a frame of reference. Try different positions in your room and speaker placements before making EQ adjustments. After finding the optimum position, *then* adjust the EQ for the best listening and monitoring experience.

What's the Best Monitor?

You'll see endless discussions on the net as to which near-field monitors are best. In truth, the answer may be the monitor that works best with your imperfect listening space and imperfect hearing response. How many times have you seen a review of a speaker where the person notes with amazement that some new speaker "revealed sounds not heard before with other speakers"? This is expected. The frequency response of even the best speakers differs sufficiently that some speakers will indeed emphasize different frequencies, which creates a subtly different mix.

I've been fortunate enough to hear my music over some hugely expensive systems in mastering labs and high-end studios, so my criterion for choosing a speaker is simple: whatever makes my "test" CD sound the most like it did over the big-bucks speakers wins.

If you haven't had the same kind of listening experiences, book 30 minutes or so at some really good studio (you can probably get a price break since you're not asking to use a lot of the facilities), and bring along a few of your favorite recordings. Listen to them and get to know what they sound like on a really good system, then compare any speakers you audition to that standard.

When comparing two sets of speakers, if levels are not perfectly matched, people will often judge the louder set as sounding better. To make a valid comparison, match the speaker levels as closely as possible. This is another situation where a smartphone's sound level meter can come in handy.

Learning Your Speaker and Room

Because your listening situation will be imperfect, you need to learn your system's response. For example, suppose a mix sounds fine in your studio, but is bass-heavy in a high-end studio with accurate monitoring. That means you boosted the bass to compensate for a bass-shy monitoring environment—a common problem in small project studios. With future mixes, you'll know to mix the bass lighter than normal, or boost the bass at the speakers so you'll reduce bass at the mixer.

Compare midrange and treble as well. If vocals jump out of your system but lay back in others, then your speakers might be *forward* (i.e., they emphasize the midrange). Compensate by mixing midrange-heavy parts back a little bit. Some producers go so far as to carry their favorite monitor speakers to sessions so they can compare the studio's speakers to speakers they already know well.

Mixing on Headphones

How you mix your music determines how listeners will hear your music. For decades, mixing was done through speakers because that was how most people heard music—a standard recommendation was not to mix through headphones except as a reality check because they distorted the sense of space and stereo separation.

However, it may be time to reconsider. Headphone sales continue to increase exponentially, and "speakers" are increasingly about Bluetooth and soundbars, not traditional stereo systems. So you need to create mixes that work over a variety of speaker systems, as well as headphones.

Headphones are not all created equal. Many consumer-oriented headphones exaggerate the low end, high end, or both—then again, that's what many people will use to listen to your music. But even with accurate headphones, music doesn't sound the same on headphones as on speakers. The sound is in your head, not in front of it, and there's no channel *crossfeed* (where your left ear hears some of the sound from the right speaker).

Before headphones became a dominant way to listen to music, I often started mixes with headphones to catch and fix soft artifacts that might get lost over speakers. Then I'd switch to speakers, with a final switch back to headphones as a "reality check." But as more people have begun listening with headphones, I've reversed that process by mixing mostly on headphones, with speakers now often providing the reality check.

I test a mix with multiple headphones for the same reason engineers used to mix over multiple loudspeakers to emulate a variety of real-world conditions. Auditioning a mix on everything from Beats headphones (bass heavy) to Ultrasone (bright) to KRK (accurate) helps create a mix that works on a variety of headphones. Nonetheless, the final reality check uses speakers. Once a mix that works on headphones gets tweaked over speakers, the mix also sounds better on headphones.

Test Your Mix on Multiple Playback Systems

In addition to testing on headphones and speakers, before signing off on a mix you should listen through anything you can—car stereo, laptop, iPad, big-bucks studio speakers, sound bars, etc.—to find out how a mix "translates" over these different transducers. If the mix works, great. But if it sounds overly bright on, say, five out of eight systems, pull back the brightness just a bit. Of course the mastering process can compensate for some of this, but you want any project to be as close to ideal as possible.

I've found Audified's MixChecker plug-in, which provides representative responses for a variety of consumer playback media (Fig. 2.9), quite helpful. If your mix sounds good on all the options, congratulate yourself.

Figure 2.9 Audified's MixChecker helps emulate what your mix will sound like after undergoing the sonic violence of less-than-ideal playback systems.

Key Takeaways

♦ Above all, take care of your hearing. That's your one piece of gear with no warranty and no return policy, and it can't be replaced at any price.

♦ There's a learning curve ahead of you—learn the room acoustics, and if necessary, learn how to compensate for deficiencies in your monitoring system.

♦ Near-field monitors can help minimize the effect of room acoustics.

♦ Speaker placement is crucial. Simply moving a speaker a few inches can change the perceived response. Avoid placing speakers against walls or in corners.

♦ One of the best investments for your music is treating your room acoustically.

♦ If you need to compensate for acoustics issues, the tone controls mounted on the rear of your monitor speakers may help.

♦ Once you've found a good speaker location that's unlikely to change, get to know the sound so you can compensate mentally for any response anomalies.

♦ Make sure that the final mix sounds good over headphones as well as speakers.

♦ Before signing off on a mix, test it over multiple systems, and make sure it "translates" well over all of them.

Chapter 3

Basics of Mixing with Computers

Mixing used to be done with hardware mixing boards, but today's music software can perform the functions of a traditional mixer inside your computer—hence the term *inside the box* (ITB) mixing.

Mixer Architecture

Software mixers have a similar layout to their hardware ancestors. They provide three independent places to adjust levels. (See Fig. 3.1.)

- *Channels* represent the audio coming from individual *tracks*. For example, the audio from each track of a 16-track project will appear over 16 channels. Each channel has a *fader* (linear volume control) so you can determine how much audio from each channel goes to the master output bus (see next). This is the essence of mixing—creating a pleasing balance among the various channels.

- *Busses* are specialized channels that sum the outputs of other channels. Typically, there will be at least a *master* bus into which each channel terminates. You can adjust the overall mix level with the master bus fader.

 See the section on "Bus Basics" later in this chapter for details on how busses are commonly used.

- The *Monitor* section routes audio to headphones, speakers, and other monitoring devices. This component of a traditional mixer often exists on an audio interface today, rather than in the recording program's mixer, but the software mixer may have a simplified version as well.

Figure 3.1 The mixer channels (colored gray), the effects busses (colored blue), and the main bus (colored red) represent the main level-setting elements in this software mixer. Like many programs, Studio One (shown here) allows you to apply colors to tracks, which can help identify them more easily.

Mono vs. Stereo Tracks

Early hardware consoles had mono inputs and mono channels. When stereo became more common, mixers evolved to include stereo inputs. A stereo channel fader would adjust the level for the left and right channels simultaneously.

With virtual mixers, there are no hardware limitations. There's no reason why all channels can't be stereo (or switched to mono operation). Pro Tools still treats a stereo track as two mono channels, but many other programs default to stereo channels.

The mono versus stereo distinction won't impact your workflow much, although it may impact plug-in effects.

 Plug-in effects are discussed in detail in Chapter 4 of this book.

Bus Basics

The most common bus is a mixer's master or main bus. All the channel outputs feed into this master bus, which includes a master fader for raising or lowering the combined level of all the channels. Its output feeds a stereo output that goes to a monitor section or directly to an audio interface, and then to monitor speakers and/or headphones.

Another common use for busses is to allow you to process several channels at once with an effect like reverb. This bus application works in conjunction with channel *send* controls, which send a selectable amount of audio from the channel to a bus. For example, if you want to add reverb on some but not all channels, you would create a bus, insert a reverb effect in the bus, and send audio to the bus from those channels where you want reverb. The reverb bus output would join the channel outputs (which contain the non-reverberated signal) in feeding the master bus (Fig. 3.2).

Figure 3.2 This screenshot from Ableton Live shows three busses with effects (A Reverb, B Saturation, and C Delay) toward the mixer's right. The Rhythm 2 track (far left) has no sends. The Melody 1 track is sending audio to the Delay bus, Arpeggiate is sending audio to the Reverb and Saturation busses, and Vocals is sending audio to the Reverb bus. The effect bus outputs and the channel outputs feed the master bus.

The distinction of busses being separate from tracks is a holdover from the days of physical consoles. There's no technical reason why virtual mixers have to differentiate between the two, and some programs treat them interchangeably. However, for many people the distinction feels logical because the two provide different functions.

Channel Strips

A channel consists of more than just a volume fader. A *panpot* (short for panoramic potentiometer) places a mono channel's signal within the stereo field, from left to right as you rotate the panpot from full left (counterclockwise) to full right (clockwise).

With stereo channels, the panpot acts like a balance control. At center, the left and right channels have the same level. Turning the panpot counter-clockwise turns down the right channel, while turning it clockwise turns down the left channel.

Other elements in the channel strip differ for different mixers. Most include equalization, input level to the channel strip, solo and mute buttons, metering, and a record-enable button. Some include dynamics processors, a fixed or variable number of sends, different ways to insert plug-in effects (see Chapter 4), level meters, and so on. However, if you don't like the channel strip options in your software, there are many alternative channel strip plug-ins to choose from (Fig. 3.3).

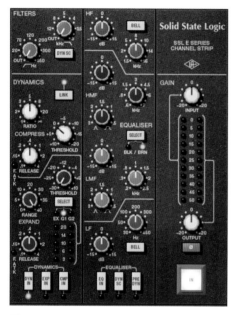

Figure 3.3 This Universal Audio plug-in emulates the mixer channel strip from the SSL E-Series, an iconic British mixing console. The channel strip includes dynamics processors and various types of equalization, as described later in this book.

Tech Talk: Mute and Solo Buttons

Clicking on a channel's mute button silences that channel. Clicking on a solo button, which is mostly for diagnostic purposes, mutes all channels for which solo is not engaged so you can hear a track without the distraction of hearing other tracks. You can solo multiple tracks at once; however, there's a special solo mode called *exclusive solo*. When enabled, soloing a channel mutes *all* other channels, even if some of them are soloed.

About Grouping

Grouping channels together into a *subgroup* (also commonly called a *group* or *submix*) can simplify the mixing process and add flexibility.

A submix group provides functionally somewhat like a bus. However, instead of combining signals from the source channels' send controls, it combines signals from the channels' audio outputs (which would normally feed the main bus). So, the subgroup represents the sum of several channel outputs. Then the subgroup bus output usually feeds the main output bus.

A typical subgroup application is mixing together a drum set's individual outputs—kick, snare, toms, hi-hat, cymbals, etc. You can adjust each output individually with their respective channel faders, but also alter the subgroup's level, or add processing to the subgroup, and affect all drum sounds simultaneously (Fig. 3.4). Changing the subgroup level can change the drums' level more easily than raising each channel level individually, which would complicate maintaining the correct balance.

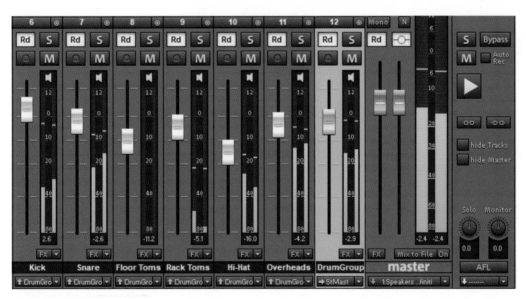

Figure 3.4 In this example using MAGIX Samplitude, the channel outputs for various drums route to a Drum Group bus (highlighted), and its output goes to the main bus (the stereo master). Note the channel output destinations below each channel.

Other musical elements that lend themselves to subgrouping are multi-miked piano (e.g., left, right, room ambiance), background vocals, horn sections, choirs, and so on.

Grouping in the Virtual World

The preceding paragraphs describe the traditional subgroup approach—now let's get modern. One of the advantages of using a subgroup with a host program's virtual mixer is that unlike hardware, where each fader takes up space, you'll likely be able to collapse the individual channels into a *folder track*, or *hide* the tracks, so they're not displayed in the mixer—even if they're still active (Fig. 3.5).

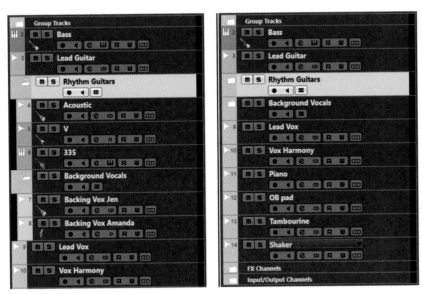

Figure 3.5 The image on the left side (from Cubase's track view) shows a folder track with three layered rhythm guitar parts (Acoustic, V, and 335) and another folder track with two background vocals (Jen and Amanda). Note how the tracks in the folder are indented. The image on the right half shows the same project after closing the folders, which makes room to see the other tracks in the project.

Because monitors have limited screen space, replacing several individual faders with a single subgroup fader can simplify navigation and mixing. Should you need to make finer adjustments, you can show the hidden channels as needed to tweak their levels, and then hide them again.

Also, subgroups can feed additional subgroups. For example, a choir subgroup could itself have a subgroup of male voices and another of female voices. Unlike analog mixing, where each submix causes a subtle degree of signal deterioration, digital mixers can submix without degradation. On with a drum mix, you can have separate subgroups for all cymbals, all toms, the overhead mics, any percussion instruments, etc. and then feed these subgroups into a drums submix, which in turn feeds the main bus.

Another Way to Group

Not all grouping requires submixing. Many programs allow for *virtual groups* or *fader grouping,* which links controls so that moving one control moves all the controls in the virtual group. Typically, you do this by right-clicking or ctrl-clicking on a fader, and assigning it to a specific group identifier (e.g., a number, color, or letter). With virtual groups, the outputs don't necessarily feed a submix—they can remain feeding the main bus. Instead, the group acts as if you bolted all the faders for the associated tracks together, so that moving one moves all of them.

However, it's important to consider how the faders travel when grouped together. In most cases, you want them to work *ratiometrically*—with this behavior, if you bring a fader down halfway, any linked fader will come down by the same ratio (halfway), regardless of its starting level.

By contrast, a *linear* response will adjust all faders by the same amount—if you bring down a fader from all the way up to more than halfway down, a grouped fader that started halfway down would bottom out, then stop and not be able to reduce the level any further. This probably isn't what you want.

Some programs can even set up custom maximum and minimum limits for each grouped parameter (Fig. 3.6), or reverse the control's "sense" so that as one control increases, another decreases. For example to crossfade two channels, one could go from 0% to 100% level while the other goes from 100% to 0% level.

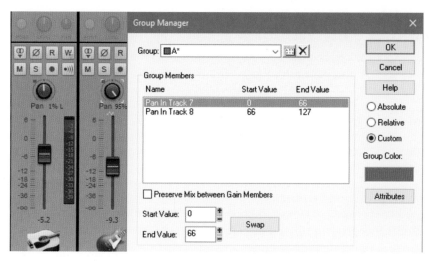

Figure 3.6 In Cakewalk by BandLab, a Group Manager sets up custom maximum and minimum limits, as well as other custom aspects. In this shot, two panpots are grouped so that moving one from left to center moves the other one from center to right.

One advantage of virtual grouping compared to submixing occurs with effects. Suppose several channel sends feed a master reverb bus, but you want to change levels on only two sends. Grouping the two channel send controls together lets you adjust the sends for these two channels independently of the other sends.

Also note that some programs can group dissimilar parameters. For example, you could group level and pan so that turning up the level moves the signal more to the left or right.

Bus Grouping

Grouping busses is also useful. If you're working on a 5.1-channel surround project and want to mix tracks down through six individual busses for a 5.1 output signal, you can group all the bus faders. Then you can create a smooth fadeout by moving just one of the faders.

Mixing is complicated enough without fader clutter that may not be needed. Subgrouping simplifies the mixing environment, and grouping allows you to make multiple adjustments simultaneously. Get to know these techniques—they'll serve you well.

Unique Aspects of Mixing with Digital Audio

Analog and digital mixing use different technologies to accomplish the same ultimate goal.

However, when working with computer-based recording, you'll encounter technical terms unique to digital mixing. Understanding these will make it easier to optimize your setup.

The Two Kinds of Resolution

Recording resolution is the resolution with which an audio interface converts analog signals into digital data. Recording resolutions higher than 24 bits are irrelevant, due to the limitations of analog-to-digital converter technology. Although you can record signals into your recording software with higher resolution, it will not improve the sound quality.

 Most engineers and musicians record with 24-bit resolution.

Your music software will also have an *audio engine resolution.* This is the resolution with which the software processes and mixes the audio, and it is independent of (and usually greater than) the recording resolution. The audio engine needs greater resolution because a 24-bit piece of audio might sound fine by itself, but when you change the signal (level, equalization, anything that requires calculations), multiplying or dividing that 24-bit data might produce a result that can't be expressed with only 24 bits. The principle is the same that you see with multiplication, for example, the product of 4 × 3. Although each number is only a single digit, you need two digits to express the result: 12.

Unless the audio engine has enough resolution to handle these calculations, roundoffs will occur—and because they're cumulative, this can lead to inaccuracies. As a result, your audio engine's resolution should always be considerably higher than the recording resolution.

Modern audio engines use up to 64-bit resolution. This potential dynamic range far exceeds anything that exists in the physical world. However, many early recording programs had much lower resolution, which may be one reason why mixing "in the box" received a negative initial reputation.

The Two Types of Audio

An audio track plays back a file—like a WAV or AIFF file—that contains audio data. It's conceptually similar to a track in a tape recorder, where the tape contains magnetic particles that represent audio data.

However, *virtual instruments* can now be part of the mix. These are sound generators that live within your software and create and play back sounds in real time—the sounds are not inherently stored in files. It's as if when you play back your audio files, a keyboardist were playing a piano along with the files in real time, the same way every time, so you can work on your mix. MIDI commands, like those generated by a MIDI-compatible keyboard controller, trigger instrument notes and alter instrument parameters.

MIDI commands and virtual instruments are discussed in detail in Chapter 5 of this book.

Of course, it would make more sense to record the piano player to capture the performance—then the piano player could go home (and you wouldn't have to pay time-and-a-half for overtime). You can use a similar process for virtual instruments, called *bouncing* or *rendering*. Particular programs might have their own name for it, like *transform to audio*. This process records the sounds that a virtual instrument plays back as an audio file, like any other audio track.

Tech Talk: Bouncing

The term *bouncing* originated with tape, when track counts were limited. For example, with a four-track recorder, you might record drums, guitar, and bass into their own tracks. This left only one track for everything else, so you'd mix (bounce) the drums, guitar, and bass tracks to the one available track. You could then record more parts over the three original tracks. The downside was that this meant you had to make sure the bounce was mixed properly because there was no "undo" with analog tape (unless you created safety copies of each recording by transferring the tracks to a second recorder, a process that further degraded the quality).

There are two main reasons to render a virtual instrument track:

♦ A virtual instrument requires more CPU power than an audio track. Once the instrument sound has been finished and captured as audio, deleting the instrument can save CPU power. Some programs can *freeze* tracks, as described later. This creates a temporary audio file, and then disconnects the virtual instrument from the CPU to save processing power.

♦ If you want to open a project in the future, the plug-in may not work with a future operating system or version of your software. If the sound has been preserved as an audio file, then you've "future-proofed" the part.

Tech Talk: About the CPU

CPU stands for Central Processing Unit, the computer's brain. It executes millions of instructions per second, from checking the USB port to see if you're using your mouse to creating sawtooth waves for your virtual synthesizer. Although today's computers are very powerful, they still have limits. Recording and processing audio is more demanding on computers than tasks like running a word processor, so anything that reduces the CPU's workload frees up more power.

The main factors that determine CPU power are its speed of operation *(clock speed),* and its number of *cores* (a CPU distributes its work over multiple processing cores). For example, all things being equal, a CPU with a clock speed of 3.0 GHz will be able to execute instructions faster than a CPU that processes instructions at 2.2 GHz, and a 7-core CPU will be able to do more real-time instruction processing than a 2-core CPU. For music applications, you want the most powerful CPU you can afford, coupled with *at least* 8 GB of memory (preferably more).

Your computer can show details about its CPU, clock speed, and available memory. On Windows, right-click on This PC and choose Properties. On the Mac, choose the Apple menu and select About This Mac (Fig. 3.7).

Figure 3.7 Computers can show their CPU type, amount of memory, and various other stats (Windows, top; Mac, bottom).

Like virtual instruments, effects plug-ins generate their effects in real time. Suppose you've recorded a guitar track, and inserted an amp sim plug-in. Although you hear the amp sim as the recorded audio plays back, the amp effect is being generated digitally in real time—not playing back from the track. The guitar track is always the dry guitar you recorded. To incorporate the amp sim sound as part of an audio track, you need to bounce or render the guitar track with its associated effect.

When mixing, I render the virtual instruments and sometimes even plug-in effects to audio tracks. I don't delete the original instruments or MIDI tracks; I just hide them so they don't appear in the mixer, and disconnect them from the CPU. This may be a personal bias from being raised on tape, but it does improve the computer's efficiency.

Setting Levels with Digital Mixers

Because modern audio engines have so much dynamic range (headroom), you can run channels at high levels without necessarily hearing distortion. However, eventually your mix will feed actual hardware, which is susceptible to overload and distortion if the levels exceed 0 dBFS.

 Digital audio is typically measured in decibels relative to full scale (dBFS), with full-scale audio representing 0 at the top of the meter.

Tech Talk: Headroom

Even modern computers and audio systems don't have an infinite dynamic range, so at some point, a signal's level could exceed the available dynamic range. To prevent this, it's good practice to allow for some *headroom,* or a range of levels before distortion occurs. For example, if a signal's peaks reach 0, then it has used up its available headroom, and any level increases will result in distortion. If the peaks register as -6 dB, then you have 6 dB of headroom prior to the onset of distortion.

Many engineers recommend keeping the master fader close to unity gain, and adjusting the gain within individual channels to prevent overloads at the master output (i.e., adjust the individual faders to prevent the final audio output from exceeding 0 dB). This is generally a better way of managing levels than keeping the channel faders high and reducing the master gain to bring the output level down to 0 dB.

It's also good practice to leave a few dB of headroom in your overall mix and not run levels right up to 0 dB. Most digital metering measures the level of the digital audio samples. However, for reasons that could make you doze off if we go into them, converting digital audio back to analog may result in higher values than the samples themselves. This creates *intersample distortion.* Unless your channel's meters can alert you to intersample distortion, you should leave a few dB of headroom to avoid this.

Loops that stretch with tempo variations can change level depending on the tempo and may cause distortion in some cases. This is yet another reason to maintain a bit of headroom.

The Best Sample Rate for Recording and Mixing

This is kind of a geeky topic, but you'll run into it eventually... so let's deal with it now. If it's too geeky, just ignore this section. The sample rate at which you record and mix will have little, if any, effect on your music's emotional impact.

By the time you're mixing, you've already decided on your project's sample rate because doing so was a necessary step to record the audio tracks to begin with. The sample rate for audio CDs is 44.1 kHz, and most home recording projects use this sample rate. However, some people believe that recording at higher sample rates, like 96 kHz, provides better fidelity. The topic is surrounded by controversy, but it's indisputable that some factors involved in recording at higher sample rates *could* influence your mix.

The argument about whether people can tell the difference between audio recorded at 96 kHz and played back at 44.1 kHz or 96 kHz has never really been resolved. (I've yet to meet anyone who can do so reliably.) Nonetheless, under *some* circumstances, recording at a higher sample rate can give audibly superior sound quality for projects mixed in the box. This isn't a wine-tasting-type difference ("the sound is pert, yet unassuming"), but rather an obvious, audible effect.

The reason for this is that sounds generated inside the computer can generate harmonics that interact with the project's sample rate. This won't happen with acoustic or electric sounds recorded through an audio interface, because the interface itself will remove ultra-high frequencies that could otherwise be a problem. But it can happen with digitally synthesized audio.

For example, consider a virtual instrument plug-in that synthesizes a sound, or distortion created by a guitar amp simulator. In these cases, the basis for the improvement heard with high sample rates comes from eliminating *foldover distortion,* otherwise known as *aliasing.*

A digital system can accurately represent audio only at frequencies lower than half the sampling rate; in a 44.1 kHz project, the audio shouldn't include frequencies higher than 22.05 kHz. If a synthesizer plug-in generates harmonic content above this limit—for example, at 36 kHz—then this signal will interact with the sampling rate to create sonic artifacts within the audible range.

These sounds won't be related harmonically to the original signal, and will generally sound ugly.

So should you record at 96 kHz to eliminate these issues? Maybe... but maybe not. Many plug-ins will not exhibit these problems, for one of four reasons:

♦ The audio coming out of them doesn't have high-frequency harmonics that can cause audible aliasing.

♦ The plug-in *oversamples,* which means that the plug-in itself runs at a higher sample rate internally. As far as it's concerned, the sample rate already *is* higher than that of the project. As a result, any aliasing occurs outside the audible range.

♦ The plug-in designers have built in appropriate filtering to prevent aliasing.

♦ The program may have an option to *upsample* sounds when converting a track with a plug-in instrument or processor to a processed audio track. This technique temporarily fools the plug-in into thinking the sample rate is higher than it actually is when it renders the plug-in output to a standard audio track (Fig. 3.8).

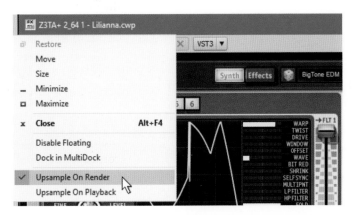

Figure 3.8 Cakewalk has an option to play back and/or render sounds created by plug-ins and virtual instruments at a higher sample rate than the project itself. This gives the benefits of recording "in the box" instruments and plug-ins at high sample rates within lower-sample-rate projects.

Because today's software can handle high sample rates, it might seem that starting projects at a higher sample rate would be ideal. Unfortunately, there are some limitations with higher project sample rates and oversampling:

♦ Recording a project at a higher sample rate stresses out your computer more. This reduces the number of possible audio channels, and won't allow running as many plug-ins.

♦ Recording at a higher sample rate consumes more disk space. Doubling the sample rate will double the amount of space required to store your project.

♦ Oversampling requires more CPU power, so even if all your instruments are oversampling internally, you may not be able to use as many instances of them.

♦ Although some instruments may perform two times the oversampling, that still might not be sufficient to eliminate aliasing on harmonically rich sources.

♦ With plug-ins that oversample, the sound quality depends on the algorithms that perform the oversampling. It's not always easy to perform high-quality sample-rate conversion in real time.

A lot of this is splitting hairs. If you have a powerful computer with plenty of storage, sure... record at 96 kHz. However, recording at 44.1 kHz has served us well for over three decades, and as you'll see in the following ultra-geeky Tech Talk sidebar, when mixing, there's a workaround that can obtain the benefits of higher sample rates in 44.1 kHz projects.

Tech Talk: A Workaround to Obtain the Benefits of Higher Sample Rates

It's possible to obtain the benefits of a 96 kHz sample rate when mixing a 44.1 kHz project. If the project includes no audio tracks but only virtual instruments and plug-ins, you can convert the project sample rate up to 96 kHz, render the instrument files into audio, then drop the sample rate back down to 44.1 kHz. The audio from the instruments will exhibit the benefits of 96 kHz recording even when converted back to 44.1 kHz.

However, if audio tracks have been recorded in the project, you won't be able to change the project sampling rate directly, which complicates matters. Here are some solutions:

When using a virtual instrument, export the MIDI file that triggers the instrument. Create a new, 96 kHz project and import the MIDI file. Load the virtual instrument and its preset, then render the file at 96 kHz. Sample-rate convert it back to 44.1 kHz, then import the rendered file into your 44.1 kHz project in place of the existing file.

With amp sims, export the dry guitar audio, create a new 96 kHz project, and import the audio file. Load the amp sim and its preset, then render the file at 96 kHz. Sample-rate convert it back to 44.1 kHz, then import it into your 44.1 kHz project in place of the existing file.

It may seem counterintuitive that converting back to 44.1 kHz doesn't cause aliasing, but rendering the audio at 96 kHz will limit the response to the audio range, so the file can't generate harmonics that cause aliasing.

Key Takeaways

♦ Although channels and busses in hardware mixers have defined functions, recording programs often treat them interchangeably.

♦ A bus is like a mini-mixer inside your mixer. Busses can simplify mixing because you adjust the levels of grouped tracks with a single level control instead of adjusting each track's level individually. Busses also make it easy to have the same effect on some but not all channels.

♦ Each channel includes a channel strip with a complement of controls that often include processors.

♦ You can group faders virtually so that moving one fader moves the other grouped faders simultaneously.

♦ Recording in 24-bit instead of 16-bit resolution provides better results. The files take up 50% more space, but most people agree 24-bit resolution sounds better.

♦ Given the choice, use the highest resolution possible for your audio engine (usually either 32-bit floating point or 64-bit resolution).

♦ Virtual instruments create their sounds in real time. To convert these sounds to audio tracks, they can be bounced (rendered).

♦ A fast CPU in your computer makes for a smoother mixing experience.

♦ With some virtual instruments and amp sims, running projects at 96 kHz may produce an audible improvement compared to using 44.1 kHz.

♦ There are workarounds to obtain the benefits of recording at higher sample rates in 44.1 kHz projects.

Chapter 4

How to Use Plug-Ins

Effects, also called signal processors, are a key element of great mixes. They can tweak sounds to blend in better or to stand out more, add interest to parts that could use a little spice, or transform sounds into something completely different. Previously, effects were available only as hardware devices. Today however, all manner of effects—as well as musical instruments—have been virtualized and can load into your computer-based music software. Note that it's still possible to integrate external hardware effects as well.

In this chapter we cover the basics common to both effects processors and instrument plug-ins; then we address aspects unique to each type.

Plug-In Technologies

Two main plug-in technologies are available for digital audio workstations: *host-based* (also called *native* processing) and *hardware-based* (sometimes called *DSP-based* or *hardware-accelerated* processing). Hardware-based plug-ins require hardware computer cards or peripherals designed for digital signal processing, such as Universal Audio's UAD platform for their Powered Plug-Ins series. Native plug-ins use the computer's inherent CPU power to perform digital signal processing.

Because native plug-ins draw power from the CPU, running more plug-ins makes the CPU work harder. This limits how many plug-ins you can use while mixing. To run more plug-ins, you have three main options:

- Use a computer with a faster CPU.

- Increase the system latency (the time required for the system to process signals) so the CPU doesn't have to work as hard. The tradeoff will be increased monitoring latency while tracking.

- *Freeze* the track. This host-based process renders the track and its plug-in processing as temporary audio, and disconnects the plug-in from the CPU (without deleting it) so that the plug-in doesn't draw power. If you need to edit the source, you can unfreeze the track to make changes.

 CPU consumption changes constantly based on the computer's current tasks, so it's important not to max out the CPU. Exceeding the available power can cause an interruption in the audio stream or even a crash.

Not all native plug-ins are created equal. The plug-ins bundled with a host program usually sound very good, but specialty plug-ins designed for mastering may give a smoother, more "analog" sound—although they'll require more CPU power.

The maximum number of hardware-based plug-ins you can run is limited only by the hardware hosting the plug-ins. Because the hardware's available power and the power required by the associated plug-ins are known, you can add plug-ins until there's no available power left—no surprises will push the CPU power consumption over the line (Fig. 4.1).

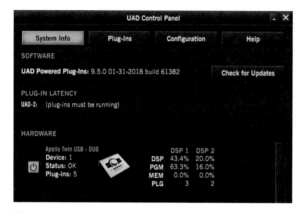

Figure 4.1 The control panel for Universal Audio's Powered Plug-Ins shows how much DSP the currently loaded plug-ins consume. These numbers don't vary unless you add or remove plug-ins.

Plug-In Formats

Several plug-in formats are available on the market today. No program is compatible with all formats.

- ♦ DirectX is an older, Windows-only format in its twilight years. Although new DirectX plug-ins aren't being developed, many excellent DirectX plug-ins continue to work, and some programs still support them. The virtual instrument version is called DXi.

- ♦ VST stands for Virtual Studio Technology, a term coined by Steinberg when the company "virtualized" signal processors as native parts of the computer environment rather than outboard hardware devices. The original VST spec was enhanced to VST2 and is currently at version 3 (VST3). VST is the dominant plug-in standard for Windows. The virtual instrument version is sometimes called VSTi.

- ♦ AU stands for Audio Units, a standard introduced by Apple with OS X. Most Apple-compatible programs use AU plug-ins, although there's also an Apple-compatible VST variation which many plug-ins support. Windows VST plug-ins are not compatible with Mac VST, and vice-versa (although a manufacturer may make versions of their plug-ins for both platforms).

◆ RTAS (Real-Time AudioSuite) and TDM (Time-Division Multiplexing) plug-ins are used only in older Avid Pro Tools systems (Pro Tools 10 and earlier). Plug-ins are no longer being developed in either of these format. RTAS was developed as a native format, and TDM as a hardware-based format. They have since been replaced by...

◆ AAX (Avid Audio eXtensions) format, which again is Pro Tools-specific and not compatible with other programs. The AAX format supports both native and hardware-based plug-ins.

32-Bit vs. 64-Bit Plug-Ins

Computer hardware and operating systems use either a 32-bit or 64-bit architecture. 64-bit systems provide various benefits over 32-bit systems. Many recording programs remain available in 32-bit and 64-bit versions for those still using 32-bit operating systems, but those are rapidly disappearing, so many modern programs are 64-bit only. It's possible to run 32-bit plug-ins in a 64-bit system (see next), but plug-ins prefer to use the same format as the recording programs hosting them.

Plug-In Wrappers

As technology evolves, older technologies can become obsolete. For example with Windows, you may have a favorite 32-bit plug-in that's not compatible with a 64-bit program.

Wrappers make a plug-in look like it has a different format. The jBridge and BitBridge wrappers allow many 32-bit Windows plug-ins to function in 64-bit Windows programs. Other wrappers provide VST or AU plug-in compatibility for Pro Tools, and so on.

Although wrappers can work well, sometimes they lead to system instability. Furthermore, as fewer people continue to use the older formats, demand for wrappers drops, so there is little incentive for companies to update them.

 Search the internet to find the latest wrappers. Most have demo versions; verify that they work with the plug-ins you want to use. Some are so old they're free, but they still work.

At a conference, the developer of a 64-bit-only program was asked about the best solution for using 32-bit plug-ins within the program. His answer was succinct: "Ask the manufacturer to produce a 64-bit version." That may sound snarky, but it's accurate.

Stereo vs. Mono Plug-Ins

As mentioned previously, most programs default to stereo channels but can be set to mono for signal sources like mics and guitars. Some effects plug-ins are available in both mono and stereo versions, so you'll need to use the appropriate version for the track's audio. Many stereo plug-ins also support mono in, stereo out configurations. For example, with a mono source or microphone as the input, a reverb plug-in can create a stereo field.

Contemporary programs generally live in a stereo world and use stereo plug-ins. If you need mono, record into both the left and right channels simultaneously, or record into just one channel, and use a mono-to-stereo implementation. Overall, the mono/stereo distinction probably won't cause you much grief, but do be aware of how your particular host handles mono and stereo plug-ins.

Effects Plug-Ins Are Always "Re-Amping"

Before plug-ins, many engineers used a guitar recording technique called re-amping. This technique splits a dry guitar signal into two paths—one routed to an amp, which was miked to record the amp's sound, and one routed directly to the recorder. To change the amp sound while mixing, you could send the non-miked, recorded sound to a different amp, and then re-record the guitar part playing through that other amp.

When using guitar amp simulator plug-ins, the audio on a track is always recorded dry. The plug-in generates the sound of an amp or other effect in real time from this audio. However, it's possible to render the track into audio that includes the effect's processing (as discussed later).

The Four Places to Insert Effects

Unlike a traditional hardware mixer with fixed places to insert effects, software is more flexible. Most programs allow inserting effects in one of four places:

- **Individual tracks.** The effect here processes any audio in the track. These are called *insert effects* because they insert into a channel, usually through the virtual equivalent of an effects rack.

- **Individual clips or events.** Clip effects process a portion of the audio within a track, not the entire track.

- **Busses.** *Send effects* (also called *bus* or *aux effects*) process all signals feeding a bus; for example, a reverb effect that's applied to vocals, rhythm guitar, drums, and piano.

- **Master output.** *Master effects* process the entire mixed output.

Let's look at each option from a conceptual standpoint, and then get practical.

Track (Channel) Insert Effects

Insert effects are named after the insert jacks found in hardware mixers, which are part of individual mixer channels. In hardware mixers, channel inserts follow the input preamp. This is because few effects are designed for mic-level signals, so if the audio comes from a mic, the channel's preamp can amplify the incoming signal to a level suitable for feeding the effect. Software mixers follow the same concept (Fig. 4.2).

Figure 4.2 Note the effects "rack" to the right of Track 2 in Acoustica Mixcraft. Opening the rack creates a window where you can bypass effects, edit parameters, control parameters with MIDI automation, and the like.

In a software mixer, insert effects appear within a specific track, affect only the track into which they are inserted, and affect the entire track unless you use automation to remove or bypass the effect in certain places. Popular insert effects include dynamics processors, distortion, delay, and doubling, but of course there are many more options. You can place insert effects in any order, but some orders are more likely to give the results you want.

Equalizers are also insert effects. However, like most hardware mixers, your digital audio workstation may already include EQ in each channel. You can supplement this EQ with other, more specialized EQ plug-ins if desired.

Clip (Event) Effects

Some programs can apply effects to individual clips within a track so the effect alters only that particular clip. For example, you might split a clip to add reverb to an isolated snare drum that hits during a big transition, or split off the last word of a vocal and add an echo to it (Fig. 4.3).

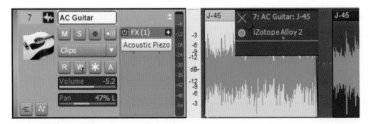

Figure 4.3 In this screenshot from Cakewalk by BandLab, iZotope's Alloy 2 effect has been inserted in a clip's mini-effects rack. This effect doesn't influence any other clips in the track.

If you add a clip effect like reverb or echo that's intended to spill over the end of the clip, you may need to extend the clip with silence. Otherwise the effect might stop when the clip ends.

Send Effects

Effects applied using sends are different from insert effects because they can affect multiple tracks simultaneously. While we touched on this in Chapter 3 in the discussion of mixer architecture, here's a more in-depth explanation.

Audio tracks use send controls to "pick off" some of the track's audio and send it to a bus. An effect inserted in that bus will process any audio it receives. The classic send effect application is reverb, where different tracks send different amounts of audio to the reverb effect on a bus. For example, if you want lots of reverb on voice and guitar but not on bass, you'd turn up the voice and guitar track send controls that feed the reverb bus, while leaving the bass's send control down (Fig. 4.4).

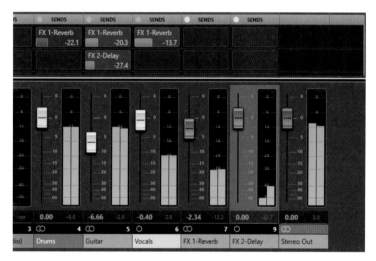

Figure 4.4 This Cubase project has two returns for send effects: FX 1–Reverb and FX 2–Delay. The Drums, Guitar, and Vocals tracks are all sending some signal to the Reverb, but only the Guitar track is sending audio to the Delay.

The send bus output shows up in the program's mixer like a channel output, but it may be called an *effects return* channel. The source track's send control can usually switch the send signal before (pre-) or after (post-) the track's fader.

♦ Selecting post-fader reduces the send output level when you lower the track's main fader. (Also, channel mute and solo buttons typically affect a send only if it's post-fader.)

♦ Selecting pre-fader will cause the send level control alone to determine the send output, without being affected by the track's fader setting.

 With a pre-fader echo setting, the echoes continue after you pull down the fader for the track. With a post-fader setting, the echo level follows the fader level.

When using send effects that have wet/dry balance controls (like reverb or delay), remember that the channel output *and* the processed output both feed into the main output or master bus. This is a *parallel* signal routing. Because the track itself is feeding the mixer a dry signal, you'll usually set the send effect for processed sound only (100% wet), and then use the fader on the effects return channel to dial in the amount of processed signal.

Tech Talk: Series and Parallel Effects

There are three common effects routings. With *series* routings, the output of one effects processor feeds the input of the next effects processor, whose output feeds the next processor's input, and so on. *Parallel* routings split the signal into two paths, like dry and processed sound, or two different effects. Mixing the path outputs back together provides a single output (Fig. 4.5).

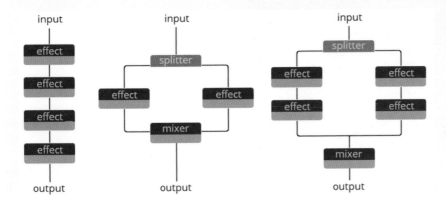

Figure 4.5 Left to right: Series, parallel, and series-parallel routings.

Series-parallel routings combine the two options. For example, you could have effects in series, and the then split the output into parallel effects. Or, a parallel split could have several series effects in each split.

Setting Levels with Send Effects

When using send effects, there are up to four places to alter levels (see Figure 4.6):

1. The channel's effects send control

2. The main channel fader (if the send control is set to post-fader)

3. An aux bus input gain (also called input trim) control, if present

4. The aux bus output fader

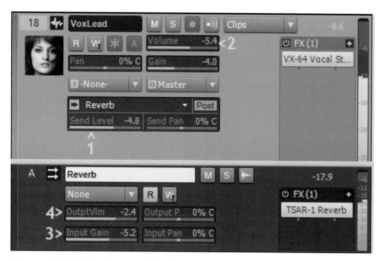

Figure 4.6 With Cakewalk by BandLab, and most other music programs, the four places to set levels with send effects include the bus and the channel feeding the bus.

Furthermore, a signal processor inserted in the bus may itself have input and/or output level controls, and the effect's sound may depend on the incoming level (e.g., with distortion, more input signal increases the distortion amount). If these controls aren't set correctly, an excessively high level may cause distortion, while too low a level can decrease the signal-to-noise ratio. Here's the general procedure for proper level setting:

1. If the send effect has input or output level controls, set them to *unity gain* (i.e., the signal is neither amplified nor attenuated).

2. Set the aux bus trim and bus output level controls to unity gain.

3. Adjust the individual send control(s) for the desired amount of effect. The higher you turn the individual send control(s), the more that channel will contribute to the processed sound.

4. Because the sends from multiple individual channels add up, they may overload the effect's input. Leave the effect levels at unity gain, and use the bus input level control to reduce the level going to the effect.

5.   If the signal going to the effect is too low, use the bus input level control to bring it up. If there still isn't enough level to drive the effect, increase the individual channel send controls.

Other Send Effects and Bus Applications

Sends make it easy to create parallel effects. Use a channel's effects send control to send audio into a bus whose effect adds parallel processing. Here are a few examples of useful parallel effects:

♦   **Wah or envelope-controlled filter.** Filtering won't thin out the main track when placed in parallel with the track it's processing.

♦   **Bass.** Keep the full, round bass sound in the main track, and send some audio to processors like distortion, chorus, wah, etc. in a separate bus. Parallel processing keeps the low-end intact.

♦   **Create stereo imaging.** Use two busses, each with a short delay (like 13 ms and 17 ms). Send some signal to each bus and pan the bus outputs left and right. This adds width and ambiance to the dry sound. Check the combination of the dry sound and delayed sounds in mono to make sure the delays don't thin the sound; if so, lower the level of the delays or increase the delay times somewhat.

♦   **Maintain consistency with doubled parts.** When you want the same effect on both parts, instead of setting up insert effects for each part, use one send effect and send audio from each doubled part to the effect's send bus.

♦   **Multiband processing.** This is an advanced technique. If busses pass only specific frequency ranges (e.g., using separate busses for low, mid, and high frequencies), then you can process each band separately to create very interesting effects. There's more on this technique in Chapter 9.

♦   **Trashy sounds for drums.** Amp sim distortion and cabinets can sometimes add a delightfully trashy sounds to drums, as well as ambiance. However, a little goes a long way—try adding a subtle amount in parallel with the drums.

♦   **Distortion.** Pick a couple of instruments to be emphasized, and send some of their audio to a bus with a saturation plug-in. Potential candidates for this include drums, percussion, and especially bass. This may also recall some of the distortion-related aspects of saturating analog magnetic tape, which we associate with "pushing" the sound.

Master Effects

Applying master effects is a variation on using insert effects for individual channels that involves inserting effects into the master output bus to alter the entire mixed signal. For example, you can use EQ to brighten up the entire mix a bit and/or dynamics to make the mix seem a little louder overall.

You've probably heard of a process called *mastering,* where a mastering engineer adds processing to a finished stereo mix to enhance the sound. Although adding master effects as you mix can help you estimate how mastering might affect the sound, if you intend to take your mix to a mastering engineer, do not insert any master effects when you export your mix—a good mastering engineer will likely want to use a familiar set of high-quality mastering tools or plug-ins.

    For more on the topic of mastering, see Chapter 12 of this book.

Using Virtual Instrument Plug-Ins

Most instrument plug-ins appear in your host program as dedicated instrument tracks (which play back through mixer channels). Often dragging an instrument from a browser into a program's main track view is enough to insert the instrument and create a track. Older software sometimes inserts instruments as if they are effects plug-ins.

Either way, three major differences apply when mixing virtual instruments as compared to audio tracks:

♦ The virtual instrument's audio is not recorded as a track, but generated in real time. Its track contains MIDI data that tells the instrument what notes to play, the dynamics, additional articulations, etc. You can use effects with an instrument track just as you would an audio track; insert them after the instrument output. Send effects, mute, solo, and similar audio track options will also be available. However, before mixing, I recommend rendering (transforming) the part into an actual audio track—we'll explain why later.

♦ Virtual instruments have parameters that can alter the sounds, and therefore affect the mix. For example, if you record a standard electric bass part as audio and later decide you should have used the neck pickup instead of the bridge pickup, you can't change that. But a virtual bass may include the option to choose the sound of a different pickup. Even if you've transformed the virtual instrument to audio, you can load the original instrument preset, change the virtual pickup, and then re-render to audio with the new sound.

♦ Because virtual instruments are driven by MIDI data, changing the data on the instrument track can change a part and affect a mix. These changes can include modifications to the velocity or intensity of certain notes, variations in the amount of vibrato being applied, or the addition of a volume swell—not just changes to the notes themselves.

Chapter 5 describes mixing with MIDI instruments in detail. If you don't use MIDI instruments you can skip or skim this information.

Instruments with Multiple Outputs

Many virtual instruments offer multiple outputs, especially if they're *multitimbral* (capable of playing back different instrument sounds on different MIDI channels). For example, if you've loaded bass, piano, and ukulele sounds, then each one will have its own audio output (probably stereo) in your software mixer. However, multitimbral instruments almost always have internal mixers as well, where you set levels and panning of the various instruments (Figure 4.7). The mix appears as a stereo channel in your host software's mixer. The instrument will likely include effects too.

Figure 4.7 IK Multimedia's SampleTank can host up to 16 instruments and mix them down to a stereo output, as well as add effects.

A mixed instrument output can reduce clutter in your software mixer by foregoing lots of outputs. However, if the instrument doesn't include the effects processors that you require to create a particular sound, then you'll need to use the instrument's individual outputs and insert effects in the host program's mixer channels. For example, many people use separate outputs for drum instruments because they want to add specific effects to each drum sound (kick, snare, etc.).

ReWire and Mixing

ReWire is a software protocol that allows two (or sometimes more) software applications to work together as one integrated program. I cover this in the context of plug-ins because using ReWire is like plugging in an entire program. Sometimes this is to take advantage of virtual instruments included in a program like Propellerhead Software's Reason.

ReWire consists of a *client* application (also called the *synth* application) that plugs into a ReWire-compatible *host* program (also called the *mixer* application) such as Cakewalk, Cubase, Digital Performer, Live, Logic, Pro Tools, Samplitude, Studio One Pro, etc. Any ReWire-compatible application is either a host, a client, or both (but not simultaneously—you can't ReWire a client into a host, then ReWire that host into another host). Although there can only be one host, sometimes multiple clients can ReWire into that host.

You usually need to open the host application first, then launch any clients. You would close the programs in the reverse order. You won't break anything if you don't open the applications in order, but you'll likely need to close your programs, then re-open them in the right order for ReWire to work. Also, although many hosts try to launch a client automatically when you select it through ReWire, if that doesn't work, you'll need to launch the client manually.

ReWire provides five main attributes (see Fig. 4.8):

♦ The client's audio outputs stream into the host's mixer.

♦ The host and client transports are linked so that starting or stopping either one starts or stops the other.

♦ Setting loop points in either application affects both applications.

♦ MIDI data recorded in the host can flow to the client (excellent for triggering soft synths).

♦ Both applications share the same audio interface.

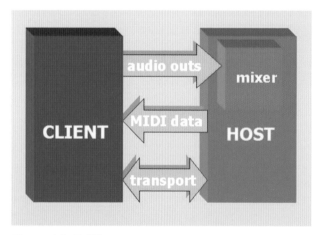

Figure 4.8 ReWire sets up relationships between the host and client programs.

Computer Requirements

ReWire is a software-based function that's built into ReWire-compatible programs. Although there's a misconception that ReWire requires a powerful computer, ReWire itself is simply an interconnection protocol that doesn't need much CPU power. However, your computer needs enough RAM and processing power to run two programs simultaneously (the host and the client).

Applying ReWire

A modern ReWire client can stream up to 256 individual audio channels into the host's mixer (the initial version of ReWire was limited to 64 channels). You will likely have the option to stream only the master mixed (stereo) outs, all available outs, or your choice of outs. ReWire can also stream 255 MIDI busses (with 16 channels per bus) from one application to another, as well as have the host query the client for information (e.g., instrument names to allow for automatic track naming).

If you choose all available outs, then you can ReWire individual instrument outputs into the host's channels. For example, if you ReWire a drum module with eight available outputs into your host, you can process, mix, insert plug-ins, and automate channel parameters within the host for each of the eight outputs.

Choosing all available outs can create a lot of channels in your host's mixer. If the channels aren't being used, it's best to delete them. Or, you can set up the client to send only the stereo outs, and do all client-related mixing inside the client.

ReWire Implementations

Each program implements ReWire a little bit differently, so check the host program's documentation for details. Here's the general principle.

In the host, you'll have an option to insert a ReWire device. The process will be similar to inserting a virtual instrument (see Fig. 4.9).

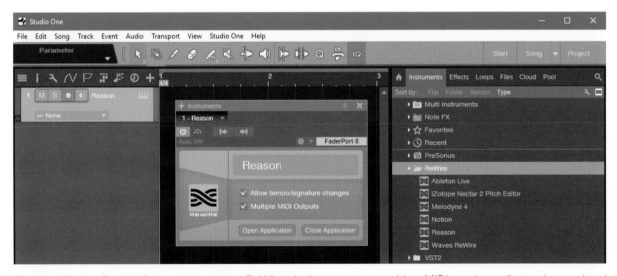

Figure 4.9 In Studio One, you insert a ReWire device as you would a MIDI track, audio track, or virtual instrument—drag from the browser into the track view.

When you insert the ReWire device, you may see a menu that lists the channels available for streaming. The selected channels will appear in the host mixer and be identified in some way—like "ReWire channels" or in the track name plus the ReWire device. With a client like Reason that includes MIDI instruments, the MIDI output menus for the host's MIDI tracks will include those instruments as possible MIDI data destinations (see Fig. 4.10).

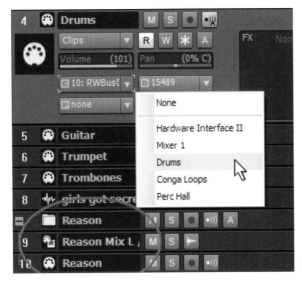

Figure 4.10 Reason appears (circled) in Cakewalk's list of tracks, and any MIDI track output can trigger the Reason instruments. In this example, the MIDI drum track is triggering Reason's Kong drum module.

Recording Controller Tweaks in Real Time

Varying parameters in real time helps give synthesized music more expressiveness. Fortunately, hosts can receive MIDI data and pass it through to ReWire-compatible clients.

Suppose you've connected Reason to a host application though ReWire, and now you want to tweak the Amp Env Decay parameter in Reason's SubTractor synthesizer. According to the chart included in Reason's documentation, this parameter responds to MIDI Controller #9. So...

1. Locate the MIDI track that your host created for Reason when you inserted it as a ReWire device.

2. Assign the track's MIDI output to Reason (if it isn't already).

3. Assign the track's MIDI channel to the desired Reason instrument. The instruments should be listed from a drop-down menu.

4. Set up your controller so that it transmits data over Controller #9.

5. Assuming your MIDI channels, ports, assignments, and MIDI thru configurations are set up correctly, you can test the connection by switching the focus to Reason and varying the controller.

    The Amp Env Decay slider should follow your motions.

6.   Record the controller motions in your host program.

7.   During playback, the controller changes will affect the Amp Env Decay parameter in Reason's SubTractor synthesizer.

Using Hardware Effects when Mixing

Software plug-ins have become so good, affordable, and flexible that it's easy to forget about hardware gear. However, many hardware processors provide unique functions. Fortunately, most programs can interface easily with external hardware, which allows for the following types of applications:

♦   Integrating rack processors (and even guitar stompboxes) with music software.

♦   Creating feedback loops, which many software programs won't let you do (for example, you could loop through filters to create resonant effects).

♦   Sending a track's output into a hardware synthesizer's external audio input and bringing the synth's output back into a channel in your program's mixer; this lets you treat the synth like a playable signal processor.

Limitations of External Hardware

If you plan to use external gear, be aware of the following limitations:

♦   Your audio interface needs to dedicate at least one input and output to the external hardware. The computer will send signals to your processor from an audio interface output, and the processor's output will return to your system via an audio interface input. So you'll need at minimum a spare input and output for mono effects, or double that for stereo.

♦   Sending audio out through the audio interface, processing it through an effect, then bringing the audio back into the interface will add latency. Some programs "ping" this signal path with a test signal to measure the delay and compensate for it. However, this compensation isn't always perfect, so you may need to adjust the amount of compensation manually.

♦   A piece of hardware can be inserted only once in a project. We've become spoiled by plug-ins where we can insert as many instances as we want... but with external gear, hey, it's hardware! If you need to free up the hardware for another track, you'll have to record the processed audio onto a track where the effect output returns.

♦   Any bouncing or rendering involving external hardware must happen in real time. Although programs usually offer *fast bounce* functions to render tracks that include plug-ins, faster than real-time processing can occur only when all processing happens inside the computer.

Setting Up for External Hardware

Host programs provide three main ways to add external effects:

♦ The universal approach that works for all programs requires that your audio interface have sufficient inputs and outputs for routing to and from external gear.

 With this approach, you assign the output of a track (or bus) to an audio interface output that patches into the effect, then patch the effect's output to an audio interface's input to return the processed signal into the program's mixer using a new track.

♦ Another approach is to configure the effect as part of the DAW's input and output setup by dedicating particular busses to specific external inputs and outputs.

 You can then call up this "effects bus" as either an insert that behaves like a plug-in or as a send to the effect that returns through a parallel path (Fig. 4.11).

Audio Connections - External FX							— ☐ ✕
Inputs	Outputs	Group/FX	**External FX**	External Instruments	Control Room	
⊞⊟ All	Add External FX		Favorites			

Bus Name	Speakers	Audio Device	Device Port	Delay	Send Gain	Return Gain	MIDI Device
⊟ AdrenaLinn III	Mono/Stereo			0.00 ms (0)	6.02 dB	6.02 dB	No Link
⊟ Send Bus 1	Mono	US-20x20 ASIO					
─o Mono			Computer OUT 3				
⊟ Return Bus 1	Stereo	US-20x20 ASIO					
─o Left			Analog IN 4				
─o Right			Analog IN 5				

Figure 4.11 Cubase (and Pro Tools) can dedicate particular inputs and outputs to an effect.

♦ The third approach is to insert a track or bus plug-in that specifies connections and levels to and from external hardware (Fig. 4.12). This external hardware plug-in might also measure the amount of delay for automatic latency compensation (which you can correct manually if needed).

 The parameters in the plug-in can usually control the outgoing and incoming signal levels, and may be automatable as well.

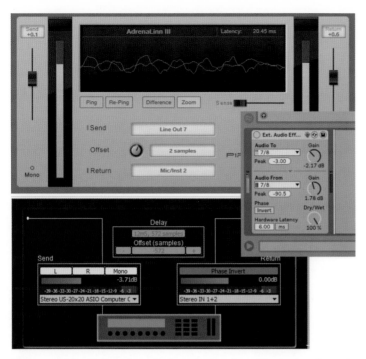

Figure 4.12 External audio insert plug-ins. Clockwise from top: PreSonus Studio One, Ableton Live, Cakewalk by BandLab.

Key Takeaways

- Native plug-ins draw a fair amount of CPU power, but there are ways to minimize the impact: use a faster computer, increase latency, or freeze the track.

- Make sure any plug-ins you buy are compatible with your system (software and hardware).

- Except for Pro Tools, VST is the most common format for Windows, and AU for the Mac. Current versions of Pro Tools use Avid's proprietary AAX format.

- It's best to use a 64-bit operating system with 64-bit software. However, it's sometimes possible to use 32-bit plug-ins in a 64-bit system, as well as unsupported plug-in formats, with a plug-in wrapper.

- Virtual instruments and plug-ins generate their sounds in real time. These sounds are not recorded in audio tracks unless you render or bounce them.

- There are multiple places to insert effects in a project.

- Send effects allow for parallel signal paths, as well as applying effects only to certain tracks and with potentially different effect amounts for each track.

- ReWire is a useful technology that allows two (and sometimes more) compatible programs to work together as a single program.

- You aren't limited to using software plug-ins. With a little effort, you can integrate hardware effects into your projects.

Chapter 5

Mixing and MIDI

Thanks to virtual instruments, MIDI has enjoyed a major resurgence. Often, the tracks in a DAW are not traditional digital audio tracks, but virtual instruments triggered by MIDI data that play in real time. These instruments exist entirely in software and use the computer to model particular sounds. They can do anything from emulate the sound of a vintage analog synthesizer to create sounds that never before existed. The instrument outputs appear as audio signals in your program's mixer.

Because they generate audio, virtual instrument tracks can use the plug-ins and mixing techniques described for audio tracks. However, you can also edit the MIDI data driving the track to change the nature of the part itself, which can in turn alter the mix. For example, while mixing, you might decide a part should have a more staccato playing style.

Note that MIDI is also involved with automation (see Chapter 11), not just triggering instruments.

Mixing's Most Important MIDI Data

The two most important MIDI elements for mixing are *note data* and *controller data*. Note data specifies a note's pitch and dynamics. Controller data creates modulation signals that vary parameter values. These variations can be periodic, like vibrato that modulates pitch, or tremolo that modulates volume.

Modulation can also vary over time through the use of envelopes, which when triggered, create predictable variations. Fig. 5.1 shows an ADSR (attack, decay, sustain, release) envelope, which can control level, filter cutoff, or other parameters within a synthesizer. This is a common envelope design that's usually triggered by playing a keyboard key.

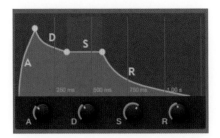

Figure 5.1 This ADSR envelope shapes the amplitude characteristics of a sound. Once you trigger the envelope, the level increases to the peak (Attack), decreases from the peak (Decay), resolves to a constant level (Sustain), then fades out when the trigger ends (Release), typically when you lift your finger from a key.

Just as you can move a mixer's fader to change levels, MIDI data can create changes—automated or human-controlled—in signal processors, virtual instruments, and more. These changes can add interest to a mix by introducing variations.

Virtual Instruments and CPU Issues

Virtual instruments often need a fair amount of CPU power. As a result, after getting a track right, it's common practice to freeze the track temporarily (which disconnects the instrument from the CPU) or bounce (render) the audio prior to mixdown so it becomes a standard audio track. You can then turn off the virtual instrument to reclaim CPU power.

 See Chapter 6 in this book for more information on freezing or rendering virtual instrument tracks.

Enhancing MIDI Drum Parts in the Mix

Virtual drum modules often provide the rhythms that drive today's electronically oriented music. During mixdown, to get the most out of these instruments—or for that matter, samplers playing drum sounds or software suites with percussion instruments—you'll want to take advantage of their many editing possibilities. This includes modifying the MIDI data feeding them, and/or tweaking how their parameters respond to MIDI data. Below are some useful drum edits that can help a mix.

Shift Pitch

A drum's pitch control parameter is one of the key ways to modify a drum sound.

♦ **Tune drums to the song's key.** Tuning is particularly applicable to toms and resonant kick drums. If out of tune, the kick can fight with the bass to make mud, or just confuse the song's sense of key. If fine-tuning is not available (sometimes tuning changes are only in semitones), as a workaround you can try feeding in a constant amount of pitch bend.

♦ **Create multiple drum sounds from one.** To play a two-hand shaker part with only one shaker sample, copy the sample and detune it by a semitone or so to provide a slight sonic variation. Detuning can also create a family of cymbals or toms from one cymbal or tom sample.

♦ **Accommodate different musical genres.** Some genres use lower-pitched drum sounds, while other genres use drums with raised pitches. You may not need a new set of drum samples—try retuning the ones you have.

♦ **Use radical transpositions to create new sounds.** To create a gong, copy your longest cymbal sample. Detune the copy by –12 to –20 semitones. Detune the original by about –3 semitones. When layered together, the slightly detuned cymbal gives a convincing attack, while the highly detuned one provides the sustain.

♦ **Create pitch shifts to accent velocity.** If the dynamics (velocity) of the MIDI notes can be assigned to modulate pitch, have high velocities add a slight upward pitch shift. A small increase emulates a drum's skin being stretched when it's first hit, which raises the pitch. This works best if you apply velocity to the pitch envelope amount (Fig. 5.2). To create a disco-type falling tom sound, increase the modulation amount and decay time.

Figure 5.2 This shows pitch being modulated by velocity with Native Instruments' Battery drum module. Amount sets the amount of pitch change, Decay determines how fast the pitch change returns to normal, and To Pitch sets the total amount of pitch modulation.

Change the Sample Start Point

Altering a sample's start point with velocity control (most samplers, and many virtual drum instruments, offer this feature) can add convincing dynamics that make synthetic sounds more realistic. Try setting the initial sample start point anywhere from 20 milliseconds to several hundred milliseconds into the sample so it's past where the attack occurs. Next, edit velocity so that higher velocities move the sample start point closer to the beginning. At low velocities, you won't hear the sound's initial attack; at maximum velocity you hear the entire attack (Fig. 5.3).

Figure 5.3 In this example from Native Instrument's Battery, the S line indicates the kick's new initial sample start point, which has been moved later in the kick waveform. In the Modulation Slots section, velocity is modulating the Sample Start and is inverted so that higher velocities trigger the kick sample closer to its beginning.

Filter Modulation

For dynamic control beyond tying velocity to level and/or the sample start point, you can assign velocity to tone so that hitting a drum harder produces a slightly brighter sound (by increasing a low-pass filter cutoff frequency or modulating a tone control). This gives extra emphasis to the hardest hits.

Hi-Hat Amplitude Envelope Decay Modulation

One of the most annoying aspects of electronic drums is often the hi-hat. A real drummer will work the hi-hat constantly, opening and closing it with the pedal, but electronic versions are often an unchanging snapshot. One workaround is to program a combination of open, half-closed, and closed hi-hat notes, and then assign them to a mute group (see below), so that triggering one will cut off any other sounds that are still ringing. However, programming a rhythm with three hat sounds is tedious, and it may not always sound as realistic as you would like.

A potentially more expressive option is to use a MIDI controller, such as mod wheel, to vary the envelope decay time of an open hi-hat sound. Using this technique, you can shorten the decay for a closed hi-hat sound and extend the decay to simulate a gradually opening hi-hat. I usually play the hi-hat note with my right hand and move the mod wheel with my left. However, this operation also lends itself well to post-processing—after recording the part, you can overdub the needed controller changes.

Mute Groups

Triggering a drum sound that's assigned to a *Mute Group* will cut off any other drum assigned to the same group that's still sounding. This is intended mostly for hi-hats, so that playing a closed hi-hat sound will shut off an open hi-hat.

However, it's also helpful to assign toms with long decays to the same mute group. Too many simultaneous tom decays can muddy a track. When you assign them to the same mute group, not only do tom rolls sound cleaner, but the polyphony of the playback device is preserved.

 Polyphony is the ability of a device to play several notes or sound sources at once.

Older samplers or drum machines often had limited polyphony. Note that toms sampled with a lot of reverb can sound like they're going through gated reverb effects when multiple drums are playing within a mute group; this may or may not be desirable.

Enhancing Synth Parts in the Mix

There are so many ways you can optimize synthesizer and sampler sounds, one could write a book about it—and in fact I will, as a future volume in this series. However, if you are comfortable with basic preset editing, here are some useful programming tweaks you can try when mixing synthesizers and samplers.

Layering Techniques

Layering combines sounds. Most synths and samplers allow layering within a single preset. If this is not available, or if all layers are already in use, you can usually layer complete presets. The following layering tips can improve how synths and samplers feel in a mix:

♦ **Add dynamics.** Layering two sounds with different velocity responses can add exciting dynamic effects. For example, one layer could have no velocity response and provide the main sound, while a second layer, with a harder or more percussive sound, could respond fully to velocity so that it plays only with higher-velocity notes.

♦ **Stronger leads.** For this technique, use the same synth sound for both layers. As in the above example, use one layer to provide the main sound with no velocity response. Detune the second layer slightly. Use maximum velocity response on the detuned layer so that hitting it harder brings in the layer to create chorusing. Normally, chorusing tends to diffuse the sound a bit, but because the detuned layer will increase the overall level when played, the sound will be bigger and fatter.

♦ **Fuller acoustic guitar or piano sound.** To create a fuller sound, layer a sine wave along with a guitar or piano's lower notes. To attenuate the sine wave at higher notes, modulate the sine wave's amplitude negatively, according to keyboard note position (i.e., the higher you play on the keyboard, the lower the sine wave level). Also keep the overall level low—just enough to provide a slight psycho-acoustic boost.

- **Bigger harp sounds.** Layering a triangle wave with a harp sample adds depth, while the sample provides detail and realism. Adjust the triangle's amplitude envelope so that it's the same as the harp envelope. Initially, set the triangle wave to the lowest possible level, then bring it up slowly to taste. Keep it subtle.

- **Add some male voices to an ethereal female choir.** For this effect, layer a triangle wave tuned an octave lower with the female choir. This gives a powerful bottom end that sounds like males singing along. To maintain the ethereal quality in the upper registers, modulate the amplitude of the triangle wave by keyboard position to reduce the level on higher notes.

- **Larger-than-life string sounds.** String synthesizers of the 70s, which were based on sawtooth or pulse waves, created rich, syrupy string sounds that weren't super-lifelike, but nonetheless sounded pretty cool. Sampled strings sound more realistic, but may lack the smoothness of analog simulations. For the best of both worlds, try dialing up a sawtooth or pulse wave and adjusting its envelope for as realistic a string sound as possible. Now layer it behind a sampled string section and the synthesized waveform will supplement the digital waveform with a smooth, analog quality.

- **Strengthen attacks.** To strengthen the attack of a sound, take advantage of the fairly complex attacks found in bass sounds (slap bass, synth bass, plucked acoustic bass, etc.). Transpose a bass waveform up one or two octaves, and layer it behind the primary sound. Add a fairly rapid decay to the bass so that its sustain doesn't become a major part of the composite sound.

- **Hybrid pitched sounds.** Percussion instruments, when played across a keyboard, acquire a sense of pitch. Layering these with conventional melodic samples can yield hybrid sounds that are melodic, but have complex and interesting transients. Cowbell is one of my favorite samples for this application. Claves, triangle dropped down an octave, struck metal, and other pitch-friendly percussion sounds can also give good results.

- **Using waveforms not as intended.** Some tweaks create entirely new presets if you apply a sound "incorrectly." These sounds may even work on their own, without layering. I've stumbled on some wonderful "electric piano" sounds by transposing electric bass sounds up an octave or two.

Taming Peaks

Synths often generate strong peaks that may create havoc on playback. For example, even though detuned (chorused) oscillators sound fat, there's a substantial output boost when the chorused waveform peaks occur simultaneously. To reduce this, drop one oscillator's level about 30 to 50% compared to the other. The sound will remain thick, yet the peaks won't be as drastic.

High-resonance filter settings can be a problem if you play a note at the filter's resonant frequency. Try adding a limiter at the output to reduce the peaks (use a fast attack time).

See Chapter 8 on dynamics processing for more information on limiters.

Synth/Sampler Parameter Automation Applications

Your keyboard's modulation wheel doesn't have to control vibrato—I often use the pitch bend wheel like a guitarist to introduce vibrato, which frees up the mod wheel to lead a more interesting existence. Also, many synths let you assign an external foot pedal to any parameter, including effects. You can use the mod wheel and/or pedal to create automation envelopes (see Chapter 11) that control the synthesizer during mixdown.

Here are several suggestions on options, parameters, or characteristics you can control with the mod wheel:

♦ **Tone.** Particularly with bass, I like rolling the mod wheel forward to reduce highs (by lowering a filter's cutoff frequency) and simultaneously increase gain to compensate for the lower overall level.

♦ **Fundamental frequency.** A variation on the above is controlling the level of a sine wave tuned to the preset's fundamental with the mod wheel. This lets you bring in a hint of sine wave for a deeper, more powerful fundamental on lower notes.

♦ **Distortion.** Some synths can control internal signal processor parameters with modulation sources. You can use offset with distortion to set a minimum drive amount, and use the modulation wheel to increase the drive. Simultaneously apply a little negative modulation to the output level to prevent a huge volume change when going from minimum to maximum drive.

♦ **Guitar-like pseudo-feedback.** Guitarists often sustain a note at high volume, inducing a second tone (feedback) that's typically a couple of octaves and a fifth above the fundamental. You can simulate this effect by tuning an additional sine wave oscillator appropriately, and control its level with the mod wheel. To be more guitar-like, add some vibrato as the "feedback" appears, and pull back slightly on the fundamental's level (Fig. 5.4).

Figure 5.4 In this screenshot, Steinberg's Retrologue sets up modulation to bring in oscillator 2's "feedback" sound, while adding vibrato and reducing the level of oscillator 1.

◆ **Waveform morphing.** At its most basic, this technique controls the level of two oscillators so that as one goes from full off to full on, the other goes from full on to full off. But there are rich possibilities, like morphing between a cello and sawtooth wave to transition from more realistic to more synthetic, or even morphing between patches.

◆ **Brightness/darkness of the overall sound.** Assuming a preset includes a low-pass filter, you can use the mod wheel to change the filter envelope's affect on the filter frequency. This leaves the attack and decay characteristics in place, but kicks the overall filter response higher for a brighter sound or lower for a darker sound.

An alternative is to vary the filter envelope sustain level—increase for brighter, decrease for darker. This will likely interact with the attack and decay characteristics, which may add another useful variation in addition to changing the tone.

◆ **Punch.** This requires an amplitude envelope with a hold control (or a rate/level envelope that can create a hold time), and as little attack time as possible. To add punch, set the hold time at about 25 to 30 ms for a short "spike" (Fig. 5.5).

Interestingly, the original Minimoogs had a brief, inherent envelope hold time—I've often thought this was one reason why Minimoogs were considered punchy.

Figure 5.5 A short hold time can add punch to a sound.

◆ **Attack.** Many sample-based instruments can edit the sample start time. Moving the start time later will take out the pluck of a string, the zing of a bowed sound, and the like. But moving the start time later can *add* more punch with instruments that have a slower attack time, like wind instruments.

◆ **Filter resonance.** You can reduce the filter resonance control to position a sound more in the background. Adding a little resonance can bring a sound more to the forefront.

◆ **Release-based reverb.** For pads, you can turn up the amplitude envelope release control to add an evocative, reverb-like lengthening to notes when you release your fingers from the keys. You may also need to turn up the filter envelope release control. Otherwise, the filter cutoff may go low enough to make the note inaudible before the volume envelope fades out completely.

◆ **Vintage oscillator drift.** To re-create the somewhat random oscillator drift of older analog synthesizers, route an LFO to one (or more) of the preset's oscillators, set the LFO for a very slow rate, and add a slight amount of modulation to change the pitch in an almost subliminal way.

A smoothed, random LFO waveform is best for this. If there's no random option, a triangle wave will work if it's slow enough. Better yet, use two slow LFOs set for slightly different rates, and apply some signal from each one to randomize the LFO waveform somewhat.

◆ **Distortion drive.** Distortion is an increasingly popular onboard effect for synths, but take a cue from guitarists and differentiate between rhythm and lead. Nothing says, "pay attention to this part!" like putting the pedal to the metal, and going from a somewhat dirty sound to overloaded screaming.

Subtle amounts are good too—I was once asked which synth I used to get "that amazing funky Wurlitzer sound." It was an acoustic piano, followed by EQ to take off the highs, then topped off with distortion. Distortion on organs and Native Instruments' Massive synth can also be a beautiful thing.

◆ **Oscillator fine-tuning.** Detuning one oscillator of a pair tuned to the same frequency can create flanging/chorusing effects. Use automation to vary one oscillator's fine tuning, thus controlling the beating between the two oscillators.

Faster beating gives a more intense feel, while slower beating sounds more ambient/relaxed.

◆ **Amplitude envelope decay.** This is particularly effective for percussive synth bass parts (and as mentioned previously, open/closed hi-hat with drums). The parameter you'll want to control will depend on how the envelope generator works for percussive sounds.

With an ADSR envelope, set attack and decay to minimum, sustain to full on, and use automation to control the release. Changing the release will alter the sound from tight, percussive effects to sounds with longer decays.

◆ **Sub-octave level.** If you don't have a sub-bass option, try adding an oscillator tuned an octave lower and set to a simple waveform (sine or filtered triangle). Automate the sub-octave level to add some beef when the song needs extra emphasis (bridges and choruses often benefit from this kind of treatment).

- **High-frequency EQ.** Most synth effects sections have some kind of high-frequency EQ, like shelving EQ, parametric, etc. Reducing the highs just a bit can help make a digital synth sound more "analog," which often lets it sit better in a track.

  If the synth needs to be more prominent, you can increase the highs.

- **Delay feedback and/or mix.** Long, languid echoes (see Chapter 9) are great for accenting individual notes, but they might get in the way during staccato passages. Controlling the amount of echo feedback lets you push the number of echoes to the max when you want really spacey sounds, then pull back on the echoes for tighter, more specific effects.

  Also consider increasing the delay amount and feedback simultaneously, not only for more echoes, but for louder ones.

Humanizing Sequences

Timing is everything, especially with music. Yet mathematically perfect timing is *not* everything, otherwise drum machines would have replaced drummers long ago. Good drummers enhance music by playing around with the time—subtly speeding up or slowing down to change a tune's feel, and leading or lagging specific beats to push a tune or make it lay back a bit more in the groove.

These timing changes are often tiny. Even a few milliseconds can make a difference. This may be surprising because sound itself moves at about 1 foot per second, so a 6 ms change theoretically affects a track only about as much as moving 6 feet (2 meters) further away from a drummer. Yet once you experiment with timing shifts, it's obvious that even very small timing differences can change a tune's groove.

When working with MIDI, some people forget about the importance of timing changes and quantize everything to a rhythmic grid. This can suck the life out of a piece of music. Fortunately, a host program's MIDI editing features can help put the feel back into sequenced music.

Before continuing with this discussion, I'd like to acknowledge Michael Stewart, whose seminal research on the topic first made me aware of the importance of small timing shifts.

How Timing Shifts Produce "Feel"

Feel is not based on randomizing note start times (but randomization *is* useful to simulate a drummer who's had too much to drink!). Humans add variations in a mostly non-random, subconscious way, so these changes tap directly into the source of the musician's feel. For example, jazz drummers often hit a ride cymbal's bell or high-hat a bit ahead of the beat to push a song (Fig. 5.6).

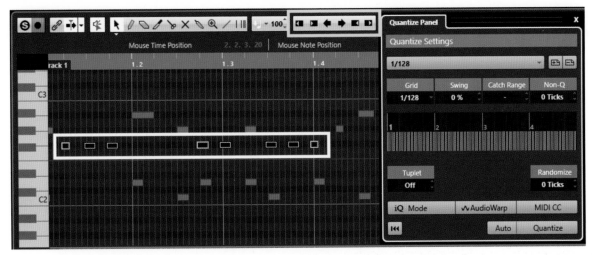

Figure 5.6 In Cubase, the highlighted shaker notes (outlined in white) have been nudged 1/128th note ahead of the beat using the Nudge functions (outlined in yellow) to give a more "urgent" feel.

Rock drummers frequently hit the snare behind the beat to give a big sound. This is because our brain interprets slight delays as indicating a big space. We've all experienced hearing a noise created at a distance, and we intuitively know that sound takes a while to travel through a big space before it reaches us.

Some instrumentalists create their own note shifts within an *overall* tempo shift. In other words, if the overall tempo is speeding up, a guitar player might speed up a bit *more* than the tempo change to emphasize the change, then pull back, speed up, pull back, etc. These changes will be felt more than heard, but just as subtle tempo tweaks can have a big influence on the sound, subtle note placement changes in relationship to a rhythmic grid can alter the feel.

Track Timing Tricks

We're covering this subject under mixing and MIDI because it's more complex to shift timing with audio. However, many of these principles apply to audio as well.

There are three main ways to shift a track or clips within a track:

♦ Click on the clips you want to shift, and drag them. Because the amount of shift will be small, you'll probably want to zoom in and turn off any snapping or grid alignment function. With longer tracks, use a scissors tool or a split command to cut the audio into a specific region you want to shift. Otherwise, you might shift portions you don't want to change.

♦ You may be able to enter an offset or start time for clips.

♦ Some programs let you assign a certain amount of shift to a keyboard or menu command. Click on the clip to select it, and then invoke the keyboard command.

Although the following applications are more premeditated than musicians playing with timing instinctively, the goal is the same—to add more feel.

♦ **What to shift.** With drums, keep the kick drum on the beat as a reference, and use track shifting to change the timing of the snare, toms, or percussion by a few milliseconds compared to the kick.

♦ **More urgent feel.** For techno, house, reggaeton, soca, and other dance-oriented music, try moving double-time percussion parts (shaker, tambourine, etc.) slightly ahead of the beat to give a faster, more urgent feel.

♦ **More laid-back feel.** For a laid-back, relaxed feel, try shifting percussion a few milliseconds late compared to the grid.

♦ **Shift individual notes.** Sometimes this is preferable to shifting an entire track. With tom fills, you'll want to delay each subsequent note of the fill a bit more (e.g., place the first note of the fill on the beat, the second note approximately 2 ms after the beat, the third note 4 to 5 ms after the beat, the fourth note 6 to 8 ms after the beat, and so on, until the last note ends up about 20 ms behind the beat). This can make a tom fill sound absolutely *gigantic.*

♦ **Avoid part interference.** If two percussion sounds hit often on the same beat in a rhythm pattern, try sliding one part ahead or behind the beat by a small amount (a few milliseconds) to keep the parts from interfering with each other.

♦ **Staccato separation.** Track shifting doesn't apply only to drum parts. Consider two fairly staccato harmony lines. If you advance one by 5 ms and delay the other by 5 ms, the two parts will become more distinct instead of sounding like a combined part. Separate them further by panning the parts oppositely in the stereo field.

♦ **Cymbal emphasis/de-emphasis.** Hitting a crash cymbal a bit ahead of the beat makes it really stand out. Moving it slightly later meshes it more with the track.

♦ **Melody/rhythm emphasis/de-emphasis.** If the kick and bass hit at the same time, emphasize the melody by shifting the bass a bit earlier than the kick, or emphasize the rhythm by shifting the bass a little later than the kick. Try it—the instrument that hits first will sound louder, even though the relative levels don't change.

How to Shift Individual Notes

Turn off Snap to Grid, and then select notes to drag them forward or backward on the timeline. When you need more precision, edit options called Nudge, Shift, Offset, or similar may be available for moving selected notes forward or backward by a particular number of clock ticks or milliseconds.

Shifts in milliseconds are pretty intuitive, but the clock "ticks" associated with MIDI timing don't have an obvious correlation to time.

The following formula for 4/4 music provides a tick's duration:

[60,000/tempo in BPM]/Pulses per quarter note = tick duration in milliseconds

For example, if the resolution is 960 pulses per quarter note, at a tempo of 125 BPM, each tick will be equal to 0.5 ms. So to move a high-hat 5 ms ahead of the beat, you would place it 10 ticks earlier on the timeline.

Tech Talk: Shifts with Audio

Except when moving an entire clip, shifting notes with audio is more complex than shifting notes with MIDI. With audio, what you need to modify most of the time is where a note's attack falls because it's of greater interest to the ear than its decay. If a sound is isolated in its own track (e.g., snare, cowbell), simply drag the audio earlier or later on the timeline.

However, you will likely find times when you want to change some note attacks but not others. Tools such as Pro Tools' Elastic Audio, or the "warp markers" in programs like Studio One, Ableton Live, Cubase, and others allow shifting note attacks (Fig. 5.7).

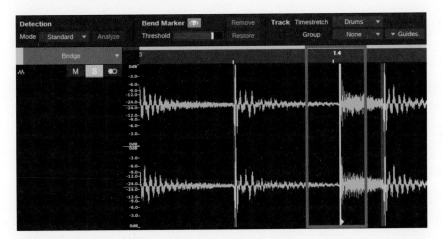

Figure 5.7 Studio One has detected the snare's transient (outlined in red). This allows it to be moved manually so it's a little late compared to the beat (measure 1, beat 4), which gives a "bigger" feel.

Quantization Options

Note quantization, which moves note start points to a rhythmic grid, is the norm for some genres of music (e.g., electro, techno). However, it's an artificial process because no human plays with 100% precision. Fortunately, most host applications have options to make quantization less mechanical.

Strength

The Strength setting is my favorite quantize option because it moves notes a certain percentage closer to the beat instead of exactly on the beat. If your timing is not as tight as you'd like, a Strength setting of 50 to 90 percent can tighten it without becoming metronomic.

You may find that your timing "errors" aren't as much errors as a lack of precise control. In other words, you may have subconsciously meant to hit a little ahead or behind the beat, but because you're not Steve Gadd, you went too far ahead or behind. An appropriate Strength setting will tame your excesses.

Start off with quantization Strength set at 50% to move notes 50% closer to the grid; then listen to the result. If the timing still doesn't sound right, apply 50% quantization again to move the notes an additional 50% closer to the grid, and so on until the feel is as desired. For example, if a note is 12 ms behind the beat, hard quantizing moves it right onto the beat. Quantizing with 50% strength moves it 6 ms behind the beat, and quantizing again with 50% strength moves it 3 ms behind the beat.

Swing

The Swing function affects the timing of pairs of equal-value notes. Each note normally defaults to taking up 50% of the total duration of both notes. Adding swing delays the second note of the pair, moving it later than the midpoint by the swing amount. This imparts the feel found in shuffles, some jazz tunes, and a lot of hip-hop.

When applying Swing, even though you're still quantizing to a grid, the grid will have a more human feel. (Note: Some programs specify swing as the percentage of the difference, for example, 4% instead of 54%.) Even small amounts of swing, like 52%, can give songs a better groove. And speaking of grooves...

Groove Quantizing

Sometimes two parts, like an ostinato 1/8th-note synthesizer pattern and a drum part played by a live drummer, may "fight." Unless the drummer is a machine, the timing between the synth and drums will be a bit off—the synth's rhythm will be perfect, while the drummer will naturally play with more of a groove.

In this case, you'll want to quantize the synth pattern to the drummer's rhythm, not the grid. This is called *groove quantizing*; the process for implementing it varies among hosts (Fig. 5.8).

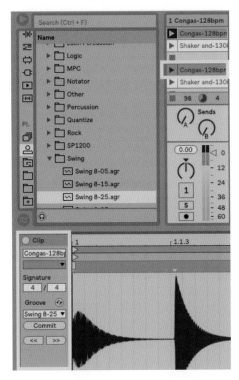

Figure 5.8 Ableton Live has groove presets accessible in the Browser (outlined in red [top left]), although you can also extract your own grooves from audio or MIDI. Dragging a groove on top of a clip (outlined in light blue [top right]) alters the clip's timing. When displaying the clip, you can see the chosen groove (outlined in yellow [bottom left]), choose different grooves, and "commit" the groove so that it becomes a part of the clip instead of being an overlay on it.

Some programs offer *groove templates* with pre-programmed grooves. Others may include a function that quantizes a MIDI track to a rhythmic reference provided by other MIDI events or timing events extracted from an audio track. A program does the latter by analyzing the audio track, detecting where percussive transients occur, then storing those "hits" in a quantization template created in the computer's clipboard. From there, you can either save it as a groove template or apply it directly to a sequence.

Considerations for Quantizing

None of this is to say you *need* to avoid the grid—some forms of music require ultra-tight rhythms. But humans tend to play *with* the beat, not just *to* it. Hopefully, these tips will help your music flow just a little bit better.

Tech Talk: Quantization with Audio

It's possible to quantize audio, although the results are often less predictable than quantizing MIDI data. This is because audio has to be stretched or shortened to fit a rhythmic grid, which can affect audio quality. It's also necessary to analyze the audio and find the attack transients that define note attacks. The analysis process is rarely perfect unless a track consists of isolated, mostly percussive sounds. As a result, you'll often need to clean up the analysis manually, with more complex audio material requiring more effort. If possible, avoid quantizing audio. If you do need to quantize audio events, consult your host program's documentation, because the process and effectiveness varies considerably from one program to another.

Tempo Track Timing Tweaks

The tempo track for a lot of current pop music is a flat line... and we all know what flat-lining means. With some music this isn't necessarily a bad thing, but it's not always a good thing either. Songs recorded without a click track will have tempo variations that can help a song breathe. For example, here's what the tempo looks like for the Beatles "Love Me Do." Their tempo variations are quite premeditated (Fig. 5.9).

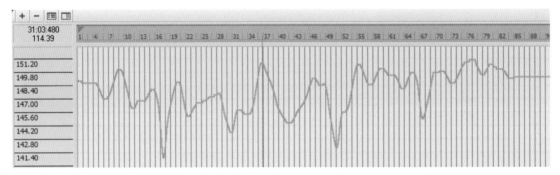

Figure 5.9 While the tempo changes in the Beatles' "Love Me Do" may appear random, they follow a definite pattern.

Note the dramatic pause at "so please, love me do" around measures 16 and 49. They didn't program those tempo variations in a sequencer—they felt the changes, and then they sped up naturally after that section when it went into the "Love, love me do" verse. They also sped up a bit over the course of the track, which happens a lot in songs recorded without a click track.

One common element of most songs recorded without a click track is accelerating tempo up to a crucial point in the song, then decelerating during a verse or chorus. This type of change was repeated so often, in so many songs that I've analyzed, that it seems to be an important musical element that's almost inherent in music played without a click track. It makes sense this would add an emotional component that could not be obtained with a constant tempo.

Tempo and Mixing

By the time the mixing process starts, it's often too late to make tempo changes because your audio tracks will have already been recorded and may not include tempo changes. However, some options remain:

♦ If a song uses only MIDI instruments, then you can change tempo however you want, at any time you want. MIDI data has no problem following tempo, and tempo changes do not affect sound quality.

♦ It's possible to convert audio tracks to a format that follows tempo changes, like Acidized files, REX files, or Apple Loops (either the standard type, or contained in Apple's CAF file format). However, few programs offer those capabilities, and stretching the file to follow these changes can compromise the fidelity.

♦ Some programs can stretch audio files to follow tempo changes. As long as the changes aren't too drastic, there may be no objectionable artifacts.

♦ If available, you can use a program's DSP-based stretching options to change audio in tracks one measure at a time. This is tedious, but if your gig depends on doing tempo changes, it is an option.

Tech Talk: About Stretchable Audio Formats

Some audio files can stretch or shorten to conform to tempo changes and include *metadata* (data other than the audio itself) that provides information about timing, duration, key, and the like. The three main stretchable formats are Acidized files, Apple Loops, and REX files. A REX file chops a file into "slices" at transients, and transparently associates each slice with a MIDI note. Slower tempos trigger the slices further apart, while faster tempos trigger them closer together. REX files do not track chord changes and are best for percussive material with obvious attacks. The Acidized and Apple Loop formats also divide an audio file into slices, but use DSP to stretch or shorten the audio. This process works with sustained as well as percussive material, and these file formats can follow chord changes. Note that with all stretchable files, fidelity is better when speeding up rather than slowing down. For example, a file recorded at 100 BPM can often increase up to 150 BPM or more, but can decrease to only around 90 BPM before audible artifacts occur.

Inserting "Time Traps"

One tempo track technique that's possible when mixing, even if the audio tracks have already been recorded, is inserting sudden, very short tempo drops to add a slight pause and build anticipation/tension in strategic places (Fig. 5.10).

Figure 5.10   Short, deep tempo reductions can add a dramatic pause without having to move any recorded MIDI (or audio) parts.

Suppose you want to add an almost subliminal dramatic pause at some point, like just before a booming snare drum hit heralds the start of the chorus. Because the listener expects the section to start on the beat, even a tiny pause can add significant tension before the release.

Although you could shift your tracks over a bit or insert some space, it's much easier to do a radical tempo drop (e.g., from 120 to 50 bpm) for a fraction of a beat where you want the dramatic pause. This sloooooows everything down enough to add the pause. (Ideally, you'd want a sound that sustains over the pause—silence, a pad, held note, etc. but that will often be what's happening anyway.)

Proofing MIDI Sequences

Sometimes a MIDI part just doesn't feel quite right. The problem could lie deep within the MIDI data stream due to small errors that may not be obvious by themselves. But when these imperfections are added together during the mixdown process, even small issues can detract from the tune's ability to sound rhythmically and sonically tight.

Typical glitches you might encounter with MIDI data are:

♦ Double triggers caused by two quantized notes landing on the same beat.

♦ Excessive or unwanted controller data that interferes with timing.

♦ The end of one note overlapping the beginning of the next note with instruments that should be playing a single-note line (e.g., bass, wind instruments).

♦ Voice stealing that cuts off notes abruptly when an instrument runs out of polyphony.

Although a group of instruments playing together will often mask these problems, they nonetheless detract from a piece's overall quality. Fortunately, the same technology that created these problems can also help minimize them—you can tweak a sequenced track while mixing, long after the actual recording took place. Before getting too deep into the mix, take the time to "proof" MIDI data, much like you would use spelling or grammar checkers to proof a word processing document before printing it. Some programs have de-glitching functions that remove duplicate notes, remove all notes shorter than a certain duration or below a certain velocity, filter out particular types of data (e.g., aftertouch that a keyboard may have generated but a synthesizer doesn't recognize), and the like.

 These de-glitching functions can be particularly valuable when cleaning up MIDI guitar tracks, which often exhibit low-velocity and/or low-duration "ghost" notes.

A more subtle problem is that sometimes a keyboard's pitch bend and mod wheels mount on the same support bar, so moving one wheel energetically can cause the other to move slightly. Check the data for pitch bend and mod wheel, and delete any unintended data.

Key Takeaways

- If you plan to use lots of virtual instruments, buy the most powerful computer possible.

- Use MIDI data to alter instrument parameters in ways that enhance the mix.

- Layering instruments can give full, rich sounds.

- Most instrument parameters are automatable.

- Although it's convenient to quantize notes to a rhythmic grid, subtle timing changes can humanize music and make it sound more natural.

- Quantization offers various options other than strict, rhythmic quantization.

- Even at the mixing stage, it's possible to apply some tempo track edits.

- It's helpful to examine MIDI tracks and make sure they don't contain extraneous data.

Chapter 6

Preparing for the Mix

This is the book's heart. You build a mix over time by making multiple edits and adjustments; what makes mixing difficult is that these edits interact. Change a track's equalization (tone quality), and you also change the level because you're boosting or cutting some element of the sound. Alter a sound's stereo location, and you may need to shift the ambiance or equalization. Think of a mix as like an audio combination lock—when all the elements hit the right combination, you end up with a good mix. Listen as critically as possible because if you don't fix something that bothers you, it will forever bother you every time you hear the mix.

This is also a good time to import some superbly mixed, commercially recorded tracks, so that as you proceed, you can easily compare your mix to these reference recordings. Note that any commercial tracks will have been mastered, so they'll likely sound louder. You can attend to this during the mastering process. For now, concentrate on the balance among the instruments so that nothing dominates if it shouldn't, or sits too demurely in the background if it needs to be more upfront.

Mixing is not only an art, it's the ultimate arbiter of how your music sounds. A good mix can bring out the best in your music, while a bad mix can obscure it. An effective mix will do the following:

- ♦ Spotlight a composition's most important musical elements.

- ♦ Keep the listener engaged by finding the right balance of groove and surprise.

- ♦ Balance tracks so that no track gets lost or becomes overbearing.

- ♦ Make full use of the audio spectrum by not over– or under–emphasizing specific frequency ranges.

- ♦ Sound good on any system—from a smartphone speaker to an audiophile's dream setup.

Translating a collection of tracks into a cohesive song isn't easy—mixing requires the same level of creativity and experience as any part of the musical process.

Before You Mix

Although this book isn't about tracking, preparation for the mix should have begun when you started recording—so at least keep this in mind for future projects. Part of your preparation involves recording the cleanest possible signal.

♦ Eliminate as many active stages as possible between source and recorder.

♦ Remove any hardware devices set to "bypass." They may not be adding any effect, but they remain in the signal path and can possibly degrade sound quality to some degree.

♦ Change strings, check intonation, and oil the kick drum pedal if it squeaks.

♦ Avoid sending line-level signals through mic preamps. If possible, send line-level sounds directly into your audio interface's line inputs.

♦ For mic signals, consider using an ultra-high quality outboard preamp and patching that directly into an audio interface line input. This can give better results than using an audio interface's onboard preamps (although most modern audio interfaces—even inexpensive ones—have very good specs).

The goal should always be to record with the highest possible fidelity, which recording engineers refer to as "getting it right at the source." Although you may not hear much of a difference when monitoring a single instrument, with multiple tracks the cumulative effect of stripping the signal path to its essentials can improve a mix's clarity.

Mental Preparation, Organization, and Setup

Mixing requires concentration and can be tedious, so set up your computer's workspace as efficiently as possible. Specific window layouts are particularly helpful because you can switch with a couple mouse clicks among different mixer views, sets of channels, and so on. If possible, consider assigning various layouts to keyboard shortcuts for added convenience.

Although features that improve efficiency are welcome, no matter how efficiently you work it's crucial to take periodic breaks and rest your ears. You'll have a fresher perspective when the break is over. Even a couple minutes of downtime can restore your objectivity, and paradoxically, help you complete a mix faster.

Many people make adjustments while tracking so that when it's time to mix, levels, panning, and processing are already close to the desired settings. Personal bias alert: aside from signal processing like EQ and dynamics control settings, I prefer to "re-boot" and start a mix from scratch. This means setting the master fader to 0 to make best use of the system's headroom, and adjusting levels with the channel faders.

If you need to reduce overall levels during the mixing process, you can temporarily group all your channel faders and reduce them in tandem, rather than lower the master level.

I set all channel panpots to mono and channel fader levels to some nominal setting, like −10 dB. Starting with a mono mix helps reveal which instruments conflict with each other. If every instrument sounds distinct in the mix when set to mono, then creating a stereo mix will make the result just that much better.

Review the Tracks

Next up: do the prep work needed to sail through the mixing process.

Organize Your Mixer Space

Name all the tracks ("Record 1" is not a name). Group sounds logically, such as by placing the drum sounds on consecutive channels, and organize your mixing console for a good flow. For example, I place all the drum tracks to the mixer's left. Moving to the right, I'll have percussion, bass, guitars, keyboards, vocals, and sound effects/miscellaneous. The order doesn't really matter, but consistency does because it makes finding tracks second nature.

Some mixers prefer not to colorize tracks because they find it distracting, but I use color–coding a lot. In my mixer, all the guitar tracks are blue, and all the vocal tracks are green. Drums are red, percussion yellow, and so on. However, I'll use a different shade for the lead guitar and lead vocal, or I'll change the shade for a track that requires attention.

For programs that support track icons, I make sure all tracks have their appropriate icons. This helps me locate tracks rapidly in big projects (Fig. 6.1).

Figure 6.1 The console in Cakewalk by BandLab supports color and track icons for those who prefer images over text.

Put on Headphones and Listen for Glitches

Fixing glitches is a left-brain activity, as opposed to the right-brain creativity involved in mixing. As mentioned before, switching between these two modes can hamper creativity, so do as many needed fixes as possible—erase glitches, fix bad notes, remove scratch tracks, and the like—before you start mixing.

Solo each track and listen to it from beginning to end; it's easier to hunt down and fix glitches when listening to a track in isolation. While this can be time-consuming, listening to each track is worth the effort. Glitches that aren't caught can detract from a mix even if you don't hear them consciously.

Proof the MIDI tracks, as mentioned in the previous chapter. With audio tracks, listen for any spurious noises just before or after audio appears (mic handling sounds if the vocalist likes using a hand-held mic, a vibrating string on a guitar, hum from a bass amp, etc.). It's amazing how many noises you'll hear on vocal tracks, like clicks from someone moving their tongue prior to singing. These low-level glitches may not seem audible, but they add up and can detract from a mix.

It's usually easy to edit audio. Zoom way in, adjust the track height for a comfortable view, then select the particular piece of audio that needs fixing (typically by dragging across it). For artifacts that you need to remove completely, simply delete the selected range. For other issues, choose among the various audio processing options based not on plug-ins, but the program's DSP (change gain, normalize, and the like).

Render Soft Synths as Audio Tracks

If you're sequencing virtual instruments via MIDI, consider converting them to hard disk audio tracks. As mentioned in Chapter 3, this will free up DSP processing power and save these audio tracks in your song's audio folder to help "future proof" the song. Although you can also freeze tracks to save CPU power, rendering always feels more permanent and foolproof to me.

When removing virtual instruments to save CPU power, note that the MIDI tracks driving the instruments place almost no strain on your CPU, so you might as well leave them in your project. Save the instrument preset in the same folder as your song project. If you later need to edit the instrument sound, then insert the instrument, load the preset, tweak it, and trigger the instrument with the MIDI track.

Set Up a Relative Level Balance Among the Tracks

Now that your preparations are out of the way, you can start setting levels. Don't add any processing yet, unless you added it while tracking because it was an essential element that influenced other tracks (e.g., dotted eighth-note delay for an EDM percussion track). Concentrate on the overall effect of hearing the tracks by themselves, and then work on a good balance among the tracks; don't become distracted by detail work. With a good mix, the tracks should sound good by themselves—but sound even better when interacting with the other tracks.

I still recommend keeping the audio panned to mono for now, at least until after you've adjusted the EQ.

Key Takeaways

♦ Mixing requires concentration, and it's important to prepare for the mixing process.

♦ Be sure to organize your mixing console so that all the tracks are arranged logically.

♦ Solo each track, and listen on headphones from start to finish to hear any glitches you might otherwise miss. Eliminate as many problems as possible because even at low levels they can detract from a mix.

♦ Proof the MIDI tracks to check for extraneous data (as mentioned in Chapter 5).

♦ Render soft synths as audio tracks to save on CPU power and also to help future–proof the tracks.

♦ Start your mix with the tracks panned to mono; if you can differentiate among all the tracks in mono, they'll sound that much better when you open up the stereo spread.

Chapter 7

Adjusting Equalization

The audio spectrum has only so much space, and each sound should occupy its own turf without fighting other parts. Equalization (EQ), which alters timbre and tone, can sculpt each track's frequency response so it takes up its own part of the audio spectrum. Next to level, EQ is probably the most important part of the mixing process—changing EQ even slightly for just one instrument can affect the entire mix, for better or worse.

Overview

An equalizer stage emphasizes (boosts) and/or de-emphasizes (cuts) certain frequencies to change a track's timbre, with the amount of boost or cut measured in decibels (dB). A typical equalizer processor contains multiple stages.

Tech Talk: Understanding the decibel (dB)

This unit of measurement for audio levels is analogous to how an inch or meter measures length. A 1 dB change is supposedly the smallest audio level difference a human can hear. A dB spec can also have a – or + sign. For example, an equalizer band with a setting of –12 dB creates more of a cut than a setting of –6 dB; a setting of +2 dB would create a slight boost, and +10 dB would give a major boost.

Equalization added to one track may affect other tracks—if you boost a guitar part's midrange, it could conflict with vocals, piano, and other instruments that have a strong midrange component. Or if you add more treble to a bass part so that it cuts through better on smaller speakers, you'll need to make sure it doesn't fight with the low end of a rhythm guitar.

Sometimes boosting a frequency for one instrument implies cutting the same region in another instrument so they complement each other. For example, if the bass and kick drum conflict, a common solution is to trim the kick's low end to make room for the bass, but then boost the kick's high frequencies so that the "clack" of the beater hitting the drumhead becomes more prominent. The ear fills in the kick sound because the hit is well defined. In some cases, the reverse also works—trimming some low end from the bass and boosting its highs.

However, because most equalizers have automatable parameters, the program can remember any frequency response moves you make during the mix. For instance, suppose you've recorded a singer/songwriter with guitar. During vocals, you can cut the guitar's midrange a bit in the vocal frequencies so that the voice stands out more. When the singer isn't singing, you can bring the guitar's midrange back up to fill out the mix.

 See Chapter 11 of this book for details on using automation in your mix.

Because EQ can help dramatize differences among instruments and create a more balanced overall sound, it helps to adjust EQ on the most important song elements first (typically vocals, drums, and bass). Once these lock together and claim their spaces in the frequency spectrum, you can deal with the more supportive parts. Drums are particularly important because they cover so much range, from the kick's low frequency thud to the cymbals' high frequency sheen. Because drums tend to be upfront in today's mixes, it's sometimes best to work on the drums first, and then find holes in the audio spectrum for the other instruments.

Think of the song as a frequency spectrum. Decide where you want the various parts to sit and what their prominence should be relative to other parts.

Equalizer Responses

Equalizers use filter circuits that pass certain frequencies and reject others. Let's look at the most common filter responses.

♦ Low-pass response (Fig. 7.1). Also called a high-cut response, this filter passes all frequencies below a certain cutoff frequency (where the filtering action starts to take place).

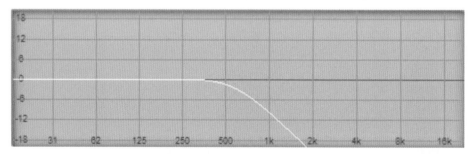

Figure 7.1 Low-pass filter response. The response drops off at higher frequencies.

♦ High-pass response (Fig. 7.2). Also called a low-cut response, this filter passes all frequencies above a particular cutoff frequency.

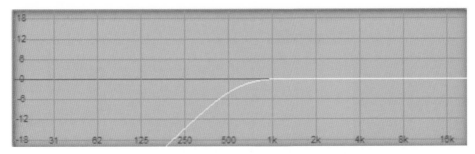

Figure 7.2 High-pass filter response. The response drops off at lower frequencies.

Note that with both low-pass and high-pass responses, the frequency response doesn't just stop at the cutoff frequency but rolls off at a certain slope, specified in decibels per octave. For example, a 24 dB/octave slope is steeper than a 6 dB/octave slope, so the response drops off faster (Fig. 7.3).

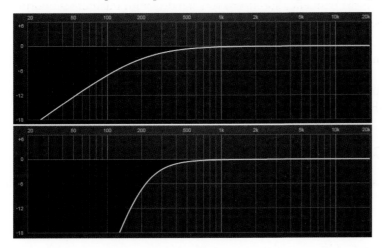

Figure 7.3 The upper high-pass filter slope rolls off response at 6 dB/octave, while the lower slope rolls off response at 24 dB/octave.

♦ High-shelf response (Fig. 7.4). This starts boosting or cutting the highs at a particular frequency, then levels off to a constant amount of boost or cut.

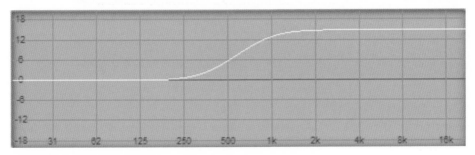

Figure 7.4 This high shelf is boosting the high frequencies.

♦ Low-shelf response (Fig. 7.5). This starts boosting or cutting the lows at a particular frequency, then levels off to a constant amount of boost or cut.

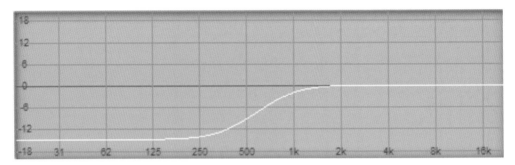

Figure 7.5 This low shelf is cutting the low frequencies.

♦ Peak/dip or parametric response (Fig. 7.6). This response boosts or cuts only those frequencies around its resonant frequency. The range of frequencies affected by the peak or dip is called the *bandwidth*.

Peak is also called *bandpass* or *bell*, while other names for dip are *band reject* or *notch*.

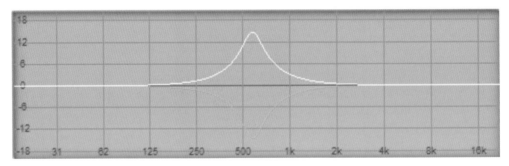

Figure 7.6 Peak/dip filter response. The white curve (top) shows a peak response at a particular frequency, while the orange curve (bottom) shows the response cut at the same frequency.

♦ Graphic equalizer (Fig. 7.7). Although more commonly associated with live sound, this equalizer response divides the frequency spectrum into multiple bands, with the ability to boost or cut response within each band. Compared to other equalizer types, graphic EQs make applying tonal tweaks fast and easy—just move the sliders.

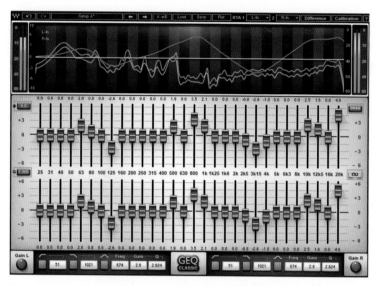

Figure 7.7 This graphic EQ from Waves provides 30 frequency bands with boost/cut sliders, as well as a parametric bell response and both high-pass and low-pass filters. With a touch screen, you can draw the desired frequency curve.

Depending on the instrument and track characteristics, all these filter types have their uses. Therefore, equalizers often include multiple bands and offer different response options. For example, a four-band equalizer might have two parametric stages, a band that can switch between low-shelf or low-pass response, and another band that can switch between high-shelf or high-pass response. However, this is not a given—equalizers can have more or fewer bands, and each band may offer only one type of response or multiple types of responses.

 If possible, avoid quasi-parametric EQ stages that include frequency and boost/cut controls, but no bandwidth (or Q) control. Being able to edit bandwidth is essential to getting the most out of EQ.

Main EQ Parameters

There are three main equalizer parameters:

♦ Frequency sets the specific part of the audio spectrum where boosting or cutting occurs.

♦ Boost/cut (peak/dip) determines the amplitude over the selected frequency range—whether the signal is louder or softer compared to a flat response.

♦ Bandwidth, resonance, or Q determines the frequency range of the boosting or cutting action. Narrow bandwidth settings affect a small part of the audio spectrum, while broad settings process a wider range (see Fig. 7.8). Shelf, high-pass, and low-pass responses may or may not have bandwidth settings.

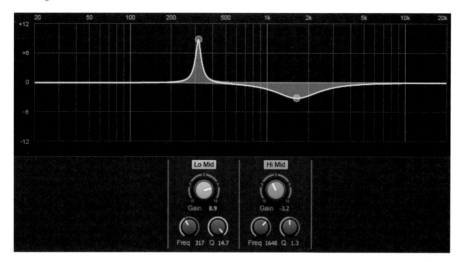

Figure 7.8 The three main parameters of a parametric equalizer. The Low Mid band (left) is boosting with a narrow Q at 317 Hz, while the Hi Mid band (right) is cutting with a broad Q at 1,648 Hz.

There are two main ways to adjust the EQ's controls. One is the traditional method of moving knobs (albeit virtual ones) to change parameters. Another option involves EQs that display a frequency response graph, where you drag nodes (dots on the graph) to the desired frequency and amplitude. With this kind of graphic interface, it's common to use a mouse scroll wheel (or keyboard shortcut with mouse dragging) to change the bandwidth. Figure 7.9 shows PSP Audioware's MasterQ2, which offers both ways of adjusting the response.

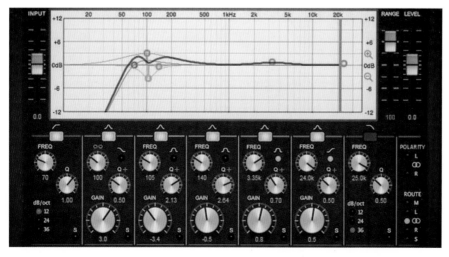

Figure 7.9 This EQ allows editing with knobs, draggable nodes, or both.

However, one of the most useful equalizer controls is the bypass switch or button. It's important to compare the unequalized and equalized sounds as a reality check. Use the minimum amount of equalization necessary; just a few dB of change can make a big difference. Also, avoid "iterative" EQ tweaking where the lows seem thin so you boost the bass, but now the highs don't seem clear so you boost the highs, and so on. If, for example, the vocal sounds thin, instead of boosting the bass, try cutting back the highs slightly and raising the overall vocal level.

Dynamic Equalization

Dynamic EQ specifies a threshold for a particular frequency range. If the audio in that range passes over the threshold, then the EQ either boosts or cuts, depending on which you've specified (Fig. 7.10).

Figure 7.10   The Dynamic EQ module from iZotope's Ozone 8 offers five different EQ types, along with a Threshold control for setting when the EQ kicks in.

With vocals, you could use a static EQ to boost the "intelligibility" frequencies, but follow this by a stage of dynamic EQ that reduces "s" sounds if the audio exceeds a certain level—somewhat like de-essing. Dynamic EQ can also tame cymbals and high-hats that are too prominent in a drum loop, as well as synthesizer patches with significant filter resonance. If a note coincides with the resonant frequency, then there will be a massive boost. Applying dynamic EQ to only this frequency reduces the signal's level if it exceeds the threshold, but doesn't affect the overall synth sound.

The next chapter describes multiband compression, which seems similar. However, multiband compression divides the frequency spectrum into bands like a graphic equalizer, whereas dynamic equalization can use any of the equalizer types described so far.

Spectrum Analysis

Many equalizers include *spectrum analyzers* superimposed on the main frequency graph. These show the level of an audio signal in multiple bands, and can be helpful diagnostic tools for showing where there are response peaks and dips. They can also show how equalization changes the response (Fig. 7.11). For example, if you see that there's a big peak in the bass range, you can reduce the response at that frequency.

With some EQs, the spectrum analysis is basic and is more like eye candy. Other EQs have sophisticated spectrum analysis with variable numbers of bands, levels of precision, display options, and averaging to show how the spectrum varies over time.

Figure 7.11   PreSonus Studio One's Pro EQ includes a spectrum analyzer with several display modes.

Tech Talk: How to Adjust Spectrum Response Parameters

Spectrum analyzers vary greatly in terms of their adjustable parameters, from simple—you can't adjust anything—to multiple parameters for customizing the analysis and display process. If you want to get deep into spectrum analysis, here are some of the most common parameters:

- **FFT size** determines the number of samples per band. Higher values, like 16K or 32K, catch narrow peaks that might not be seen with smaller FFT sizes, and give better frequency resolution. The tradeoff is that it might take longer to compute the display.

- **FFT overlap** sets the amount by which the analysis bands overlap. Higher values (50% and above) provide a more accurate analysis, but slow down response.

- **Smoothing window** determines the analysis algorithm. Different algorithms trade off sharpness of peaks and leakage between neighboring bands (i.e., data in one band influences the ones next to it). Triangular is a compromise between peak sharpness and leakage, while rectangular provides accurate peak drawing but high leakage. Blackman-Harris has little leakage, but the peaks have a more rounded appearance.

- **3D vs. 2D** shows the information in different ways. 2D shows amplitude vs. frequency, while 3D displays a series of "slices" within the selected region that relate time, frequency, and amplitude.

- **Range, reference, etc.** are parameters that let you adjust the scale, zoom in on specific areas of the graph, change the 0 dB reference, etc.

- **Linear vs. log response** is best set to Log for audio work, as this curve more closely approximates how your hearing responds.

- **Maximum** retains the highest levels reached in each band—like the "peak hold" function on some VU meters.

Linear-Phase Equalization

There are two broad equalization technologies, *non-linear* and *linear-phase*. Each has advantages and disadvantages; some equalizers offer both modes, so use whichever is best for a particular application. Linear-phase equalizer user interfaces are similar to standard equalizers.

Linear-Phase Basics

Traditional EQ introduces *phase shifts* when you boost or cut. With multiple EQ stages, these phase differences among the stages can produce subtle cancellations or reinforcements at particular frequencies. This may create an effect called *smearing*, which, depending on the settings, can be subtle or obvious. However, note that these phase shifts are also what give particular EQs their character and therefore are sometimes desirable.

Linear-phase EQ delays the signal so that all bands are in phase with each other. Linear-phase EQ is sometimes called *surgical* EQ because of its accuracy. If you compare non-linear and phase-linear modes, each with a massive treble boost, you'll almost certainly consider the linear-phase processed audio more transparent. Conversely, the phase shifts inherent in non-linear equalization can provide a particular character you might like for some individual tracks or even entire mixes.

Comparing phase-linear and non-linear modes, I find their personalities are audibly (albeit subtly) different. Non-linear mode adds a bit of an upper midrange edge, whereas linear-phase operation is more neutral in how it affects the sound. Also, for a given amount of gain, linear-phase mode will sound like it has less of an effect because of its precision.

Limitations

Linear-phase equalizers aren't perfect. Because they need to delay the signal, tracks that don't include linear-phase processing also have to be delayed to play back in sync. This increases latency (delay) through the system. Unlike recording, latency when mixing isn't much of a problem. Hearing a drum hit 20 ms late when recording a part can be annoying, but you won't notice a 20 ms delay between when you move a fader and when it changes the level.

Also, phase-linear operation exhibits a phenomenon called *pre-ringing*. This adds a low-level, "swooshing" artifact *before* audio transients. Normally pre-ringing isn't an issue because it's audible only at relatively low frequencies with high gain and Q (width) settings. However with hip-hop, EDM, and other bass-heavy musical genres, you may want high-gain/high-Q settings at low frequencies on specific tracks. For those applications, a linear-phase EQ may not be the best choice.

Conversely, non-linear EQs can exhibit a phenomenon called *post-ringing* after transients. This tends not to be noticeable because it's masked by the audio that follows a transient, but it exists. Neither pre-ringing nor post-ringing are deal-breakers at all because they tend to matter only at extreme settings. Still, it's useful to understand the phenomenon so you can choose the appropriate EQ response.

The following screenshot shows kick drum pre-ringing with high-gain, narrow-width settings. However, note that Fig. 7.12 is zoomed way in to magnify the waveform and reveal the low-level pre-ringing (this is why the kick appears clipped, even though it isn't).

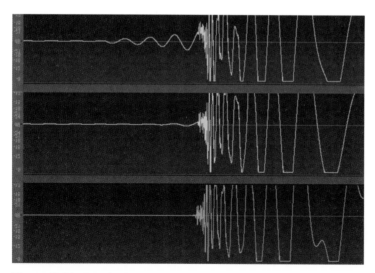

Figure 7.12 Pre-ringing with a kick drum processed by linear-phase EQ. High-gain linear-phase EQ (top) shows obvious pre-ringing; moderate-gain linear-phase EQ (middle) shows low-level pre-ringing; non-linear EQ (bottom) shows no pre-ringing.

The blue waveform at the top of Figure 7.12 shows a kick with a linear-phase EQ boost at 100 Hz, a gain of 10 dB, and a width of 10. The pre-ringing that produces a swooshing sound is visually obvious.

The yellow (middle) waveform shows the same EQ on the kick with a gain of 5 dB and a width of 5. A tiny bit of pre-ringing is visible just before the attack. The green waveform at the bottom again has an EQ with a gain of 10 dB and width of 10, but this EQ uses non-linear equalization so there's no pre-ringing. The line to the left of the attack is straight.

In most applications, pre-ringing will not be an issue, and may not even be audible. But if it is, you can use a non-linear mode instead.

Minimizing Latency

Because phase-linear operation uses a fair amount of CPU power and can cause latency, there may be low-, medium-, and high-quality options for CPU consumption. Higher-quality options aren't necessary during the initial stages of a mix. So use the low setting for the "snappiest" response, then switch over to the high setting when doing the final mix.

 Before getting too concerned about plug-in latency, first make sure the cause isn't a misadjusted audio interface parameter.

Mid-Side Processing with Equalization

Some EQs offer *mid-side* processing as well as conventional stereo processing. Mid-side processing encodes a stereo track into two separate components: the center becomes the *mid* component in the left channel, while the difference between the right and left channels (i.e., what the two channels don't have in common) become the *side* component in the right channel. You can then process these components separately, with eventual decoding back into stereo.

It's possible to "construct" this type of processing from various processing modules if you don't have EQ with mid-side processing, but an EQ designed for the task can encode the signal into the mid and side components automatically for processing, and then decode the results in real time so you can hear the results in standard stereo (Fig. 7.13).

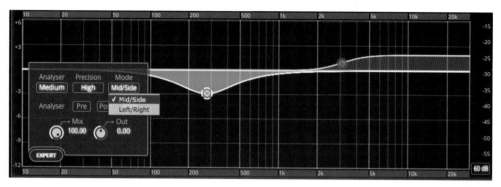

Figure 7.13 This screenshot of Cakewalk's LP EQ shows a dip around 300 Hz for the mid frequencies (the "M" node) and a shelving boost starting around 3 kHz for the sides (the "S" node).

Linear-phase equalizers are best for this application because they introduce no phase shift or misalignment between the right and left channels. This is crucial to avoid degrading the decoded stereo imaging.

Mid-side processing is exceptionally useful for mastering because it enables pseudo-remixing on a stereo track. However, it can also enhance stereo tracks when mixing. One typical application is boosting the higher-frequency side components to provide more "air" and a wider stereo image. And if you want a super-anchored, centered bass sound, mid-side EQ processing is ideal for reducing the bass in the sides, and if needed, also increasing bass in the middle.

Drums with lots of room ambiance can benefit from some upper mids in the sides and lower mids in the center to accent the kick. If a synth bass's wide image interferes with other instruments, you can use mid-side processing to bring down the bass in the sides.

Mid-side processing can also shape reverb. For the mid processing, select a high-pass curve, and set the frequency so high that it takes out essentially everything. This removes most of the reverb from the center, where it could muddy the bass and kick. Then shape the remaining reverb with the side EQ.

The Pros—and Pitfalls—of Presets

EQ presets can provide a starting point that may potentially save time when mixing. Certain instruments tend to favor particular EQ settings, even in different songs. When an EQ setting works well, save it. You can also save presets with curves that have a more generic purpose (e.g., brighter, more bass, etc.), which you edit for a specific application (Fig. 7.14). However, every project is different. An acoustic guitar preset that sounds ideal for solo guitar may not be ideal when the acoustic guitar is part of an ensemble.

Figure 7.14   This generic drum preset can serve as a point of departure, but you'll likely need to do some tweaking anyway.

There are even plug-ins, like iZotope's Neutron, that analyze audio and generate a suggested preset. These can come closer to what you want than a more generic preset, but you'll still likely need to do at least some editing.

 Presets might not be saved in the same folder as the program that uses them. When backing up your data, find where presets are saved, and back up that location. Also back up other configuration files and preferences that aren't saved with projects.

As you become more proficient with recording, it's likely you'll rely less on presets because it will take less time to create the settings you want from scratch than to tweak existing settings. Presets have their uses, but avoid getting into creative ruts by relying on them.

EQ Applications

Adjust equalization with your ears, not your eyes. Once after doing a mix, I noticed the client writing down the EQ settings I'd made. When I asked why, he said it was because he liked the EQ and wanted to use the same settings in future mixes.

That's risky because EQ is *part* of the mixing process. Just as levels, panning, and reverb are different for each mix, so is setting the correct EQ type and amount. But to do that, you need to understand how to find the magic EQ frequencies for diverse musical material, as well as which equalizer tool to choose.

There are four main applications for EQ, as described in depth shortly:

♦ Solving problems

♦ Emphasizing or de-emphasizing an instrument in a mix

♦ Altering a sound's personality

♦ Changing the stereo image

Each application requires specialized techniques and approaches. But equalization is powerful, so use it sparingly. When you make a change that sounds good, cut it in half. In other words, if boosting a signal by 2 dB at 4 kHz seems to improve a track's sound, pull back the boost to 1 dB and live with the sound for a while. It's easy to get stuck in a spiral where if you boost the treble, the bass then lacks prominence... so you boost the bass, but now the midrange seems weak, so you boost that, and now you're back to where you started.

Solve Problems

EQ can fix some obvious problems, such as an instrument with a resonance or peak that interferes with other instruments or causes level-setting difficulties. Let's look at some real-world examples that show how EQ can solve common problems that occur during mixing.

Remove Subsonic Audio

Analog consoles, and analog gear in general, rarely have response down to the *subsonic* range (below the range of human hearing). However, digital technology can create and reproduce subsonic signals, which take up dynamic range even if you can't hear them. Some modern audio interfaces have frequency responses that go down to DC—essentially, 0 Hz.

To minimize subsonic audio, insert a steep, low-cut filter in each channel at a very low frequency, like 20 to 40 Hz (Fig. 7.15).

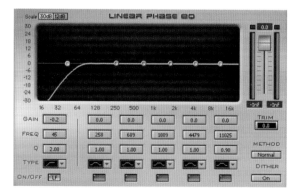

Figure 7.15 Waves makes a linear-phase EQ whose low-band section works well for low frequency and subsonic removal.

Some engineers like to reduce all low-frequency energy below an instrument's lowest note. For example, a guitar note doesn't go much below 90 Hz so theoretically, you can set a sharp cutoff starting at around 60 Hz. This may tighten up the sound if it includes low-frequency sounds that have nothing to do with guitar. Other engineers feel this is unnecessary and removes parts of the audio people should hear. Listen to your audio carefully, and decide for yourself.

Tame Resonances

Nylon-string classical guitars are often designed to project well on stage, thanks to a strong body resonance in the lower midrange that causes a strong peak. However, recording has different requirements than playing live. Setting levels so that the peaky, low frequency notes don't distort can cause the higher guitar notes to sound weak by comparison.

Although dynamic range compression or limiting is one possible solution, this can alter the guitar's attack. While this effect might not be noticeable in an ensemble, it sticks out with a solo instrument. A more natural-sounding solution is using EQ to apply a frequency cut equal and opposite to the natural boost, thus leveling out the response. But there's a trick to finding problem frequencies so you can alter them; here's the procedure:

1. Turn down the monitor volume—the sound might get nasty and distorted during the following steps.

2. Set the EQ for lots of boost (10 to 12 dB) with a fairly narrow bandwidth (a resonance setting of around 10).

3. As the instrument plays, sweep the frequency control slowly. Any peaks will jump out due to the boosting and narrow bandwidth. Some peaks may even distort.

4. Find the loudest peak and reduce the amplitude until the peak falls into balance with the rest of the instrument sound. You may need to widen the bandwidth somewhat if the peak is broad, or use a narrow bandwidth if the resonance is particularly sharp.

This technique of boosting/finding the peak and applying a cut can help eliminate midrange "honking," reduce strident peaks in wind instruments, tame amp sim resonances, and more. Of course, sometimes you want to preserve these resonances so the instrument stands out, but applying EQ to reduce peaks often lets instruments sit more gracefully in the track.

This type of problem solving also underscores a key principle of EQ: It's sometimes better to cut than boost. Boosting uses up headroom; cutting opens up headroom. With the example of nylon-string guitar, cutting the peak allows for bringing up the average guitar level, thus producing a louder sound without any dynamics processing.

Make Amp Sims Sound Warmer

Amp sims are extremely flexible, but a little EQ can create a sweeter sound. Physical amps have cabinets with limited frequency responses, so adding a low-pass filter set to a high frequency (above 5 kHz) with as steep a slope as possible (e.g., 48 dB/octave) can often warm the sound up a bit.

Amp sims may also exhibit a resonant, unpleasant whistling tonality. The frequency at which this occurs varies (and it may not exist at all), depending on the amp being modeled. A steep notch filter tuned to this resonant frequency provides a creamier, smoother, less brittle sound quality (Fig. 7.16).

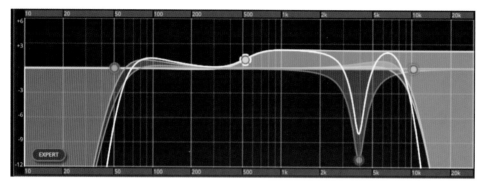

Figure 7.16 Creating a steep notch around 4 kHz helps reduce the "fizz" generated by a particular amp sim model. The white line indicates the composite curve of the four filter stages.

Minimize Vocal Pops

With vocals, a directional mic (e.g., a cardioid response) accentuates bass response as the vocalist moves closer to the mic. This isn't always a problem, but if plosive sounds like "b" or "p" produce a massive pop, that *is* a problem. Ideally, a pop filter would have been used to minimize these issues while recording. If not, insert a steep high-pass filter, and set its cutoff frequency just below the lowest vocal notes (Fig. 7.17).

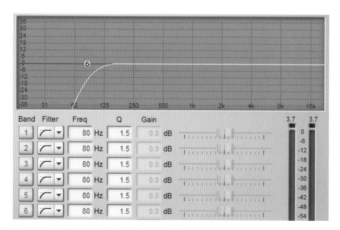

Figure 7.17 This virtual pop filter stacks six high-pass filters, each with a bit of Q, to create a response that drops dramatically below around 125 Hz.

Reduce Muddiness

Some recordings will sound *muddy,* which means they lack high-frequency and low-frequency definition. Although the tendency might be to boost the highs and lows, a better solution may be to add a shallow cut in the lower midrange, around 200 to 300 Hz (Fig. 7.18). This tightens up the high and low frequencies.

Figure 7.18 IK Multimedia's EQual is being used to reduce the lower midrange and minimize the audio's muddy qualities.

Create Virtual Mics with EQ

I sometimes record acoustic rhythm guitars with a single mic for two main reasons: to avoid issues with phase cancellations among multiple mics, and for faster setup time. Besides, rhythm guitar parts often sit in the background anyway. I then add some ambiance with delay and reverb processors to obtain a somewhat bigger sound. However, on an album project with classical guitarist Linda Cohen, the solo guitar needed to be upfront and the lack of a stereo image due to using a single mic was not acceptable.

Rather than experiment with multiple mics and deal with phase issues, I decided to go for the most accurate sound possible from one high-quality, condenser mic. This was successful, in the sense that the sound I heard moving from the control room to the studio was virtually identical. Upon starting the mix, though, the sound lacked realism. Thinking about what one hears when sitting close to a classical guitar provided clues on how to obtain the desired sound.

When you're facing a guitarist, your right ear picks up on some of the finger squeaks and string noise from the guitarist's fretting hand. Meanwhile, your left ear picks up some of the body's "bass boom." Although not as directional as the high-frequency finger noise, it still shifts the lower part of the frequency spectrum somewhat to the left. Meanwhile, the main guitar sound fills the room, providing the acoustic equivalent of a center channel.

On the source guitar track, I had applied a –6 dB cut at 225 Hz, where the guitar exhibited a strong resonant peak. Sending the guitar track into two additional busses solved the imaging problem: I gave one bus a drastic treble cut and panned it somewhat left. On the other bus, I applied a drastic bass cut and panned the image toward the right (Fig. 7.19).

Figure 7.19 This image shows how the main track (toward the left) splits into three pre-fader busses, each with its own EQ.

I set the EQ for the left-panned bus to cut frequencies above around 200 Hz, with a 24 dB/octave slope to focus on the guitar body's boom. On the right-panned bus, which was used to emphasize finger noises and high frequencies, I applied a high-pass filter with a 24 dB/octave slope at a frequency of around 1 kHz.

The send to bus 3 was used for the main guitar sound. I offset its high-pass and low-pass filters a little more than an octave from the other two busses, e.g., 150 Hz for the high-pass and 2.4 kHz for the low-pass (Fig. 7.20)

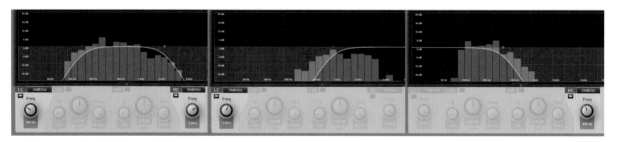

Figure 7.20 The curve on the left trims the response of the main guitar sound, the curve in the middle isolates high frequencies, and the curve on the right isolates low frequencies. Controls that aren't relevant are grayed out.

To apply this technique, monitor the first two busses and set a good balance of the low and high-frequency components. Then bring up the third send's level, with its pan centered. The result should be a big guitar sound with a stereo image… but we're not done quite yet.

The balance of the three tracks is crucial to obtaining the most realistic sound, as are the EQ frequencies. Experiment with the EQ settings, and consider reducing the frequency range of the bus with the main guitar sound. If the image is too wide, pan the low- and high-frequency busses more to center. It helps to monitor the output in mono as well as stereo for a reality check.

Once you nail the right settings, you may be taken aback to hear the sound of a stereo acoustic guitar with no phase issues. The sound is stronger and more consistent, and the stereo image is solid.

Emphasize Instruments

Certain instrument frequencies stand out, but also, the human ear is more sensitive at particular frequencies—especially in the 3 to 4 kHz range. To have an instrument stand out, boost a bit in the 3 to 4 kHz range (this is particularly true with vocals). However, if you do this to multiple tracks so they jump out of the mix, then the result will sound harsh. So, you'll want to reserve this kind of boost for the tracks that not only need to stand out, but that are crucial to the mix.

If your mix does not have enough bass, it may make more sense to boost the lowest bass frequencies with EQ than to increase the level of the instrument. Increasing the level will raise the bass's low end, but also emphasize higher bass frequencies that may conflict with other instruments.

The same technique mentioned previously of finding and cutting specific frequencies can also eliminate interference among competing instruments. For example, when mixing a Spencer Brewer track for Narada records, I ran into two woodwind parts that had resonant peaks around the same frequency. When playing *en ensemble*, they would load up that part of the frequency spectrum, which made them difficult to differentiate.

Here's a workaround for this kind of issue:

1. Find, then reduce the peak on one of the instruments (as described with the nylon-string guitar example above) to create a more even sound.

2. Note the amount of cut and bandwidth that was applied to reduce the peak.

3. Using a second stage of EQ, apply a roughly equal and opposite boost at either a slightly higher or slightly lower frequency than the natural peak.

Both instruments will now sound more distinct because each will have a peak in a different part of the audio spectrum.

Create New Sonic Personalities

EQ can also change a sound's character, like giving a brash rock piano sound a more classical character by reducing the brightness and boosting the low end. This type of application requires relatively gentle EQ, possibly at several different points in the audio spectrum.

Musicians often summarize an instrument's character with various terms. Let's correlate these terms to positive attributes when equalized correctly, and negative attributes when not—but also note these terms are very subjective:

♦ **Bass** (below 200 Hz)—Positive: bottom, deep; Negative: bottom-heavy, muffled

♦ **Lower midrange** (200 to 500 Hz)—Positive: warm, fat; Negative: muddy, dull

♦ **Midrange** (500 Hz to 2.5 kHz)—Positive: defined, forward; Negative: honking, thin

♦ **Upper midrange** (2.5 kHz to 5 kHz)—Positive: present, articulate; Negative: screechy, harsh

♦ **Treble** (5 kHz and higher)—Positive: bright, airy; Negative: annoying, fizzy

For example, to add warmth, apply a gentle boost (3 dB or so) somewhere in the 200 to 500 Hz range. However, if a sound is muddy, try a gentle cut in the same range. Also, remember that cutting may be preferable to boosting—if you need more brightness *and* bottom, try cutting the midrange rather than boosting the high and low frequencies.

Additional Equalization Tips

♦ **Apply problem-solving and character-altering EQ early in the mixing process.** EQ is ultimately about changing levels (albeit in specific frequency ranges), so any EQ changes you make will alter the overall instrumental balance and influence how the mix develops. For example, strummed acoustic guitars cover a lot of bandwidth; even at relatively low levels their sound can take over a mix (sometimes a good thing, sometimes not). So, an engineer might accent the high end but turn the overall guitar level down. This gives the guitar some percussive propulsion without interfering with the rest of the midrange.

♦ **Instruments EQ'ed in isolation to sound great may not sound great when combined.** If every track is equalized to leap out at you, you'll have no room left for a track to breathe. Also, you will probably want to EQ some instruments to take on more supportive roles. For example, during vocals, consider cutting the midrange a bit on supporting instruments (e.g., piano) to open up more space in the audio spectrum for voice.

♦ **Shelving filter responses are good for a general, gentle lift in the bass and/or treble regions.** They can also tame bass and/or treble regions that are too prominent.

♦ **300 to 400 Hz is often considered the "mud" frequency because a lot of instruments have energy in that frequency range.** Sometimes that energy can add together into a sonic blob. A piano may sound perfect when mixed at a certain level by itself, but sound indistinct when other instruments are mixed in. Try cutting either the piano or the other instruments a little at 400 Hz or so because that will open up space for the instrument that isn't being cut. Both should come through clearly in the mix as separate entities.

Key Takeaways

♦ There are many different equalizer responses. Learn them so you can use the correct response to create the desired result.

♦ When mixing, EQ makes it possible for each instrument to carve out its own part of the audio spectrum.

♦ Equalization changes levels, albeit in specific frequencies. As you mix, you may need to revisit levels when you change EQ settings.

♦ Although the spectrum analyzers included with some EQs can be helpful in locating "problem" frequencies, your ears should always be the final arbiters of what sounds correct.

♦ Linear-phase equalization can be more "surgical" and precise than standard EQ, but it requires extra CPU power and can result in more latency. Some engineers also feel it lacks character.

♦ Emulating conventional analog EQ adds a certain character to the sound. Some processors emulate the gentler curves of passive EQ, while others produce sharper responses. The character can vary considerably from one EQ to another.

Chapter 8

Adding Dynamics Processing

Along with equalization, dynamics control is one of the most important processors for mixing. Now that the tone is under control, let's delve into dynamics.

Dynamic range is the difference between a recording's loudest and softest sections. Live music has an extremely wide dynamic range that was impossible to capture on tape or vinyl. So, being able to restrict the dynamic range—soft enough not to overload the tape, but loud enough to rise above the tape hiss—was essential.

The invention of noise reduction for tape greatly improved tape's performance. But 24-bit digital audio means the medium's dynamic range is no longer a significant issue. With high-quality input and output electronics, we can record very high and very low levels. Yet dynamics processing remains a crucial part of mixing because when used correctly, it can make sounds stand out more in a mix and provide more overall "punch" to a production.

Another application for dynamics processing is to help players who lack a good *touch* (the ability to play an instrument with controlled nuances). For example, a singer with really good mic technique moves closer or farther away from the mic to keep relatively constant levels. An inexperienced singer with less developed technique might create level variations that, unlike level changes designed to enhance the music, could cause some words to drop out or certain passages to be uneven. Dynamics processing can help compensate for these issues.

Bassists often use compression because the ear is less sensitive in the bass range, so subtle dynamics tend to get lost. Evening out the bass's dynamic range provides a fuller low end, which makes it easier to hear the bass part. Restricting dynamic range to make soft parts louder can also bring music above the background noise of everyday life, like road noise when listening in cars.

Commercials use a particularly sadistic variant on dynamics control to make the perceived loudness as high as humanly possible. Soundtracks alter dynamics to keep music from competing too much with dialog, and broadcasting controls dynamics to prevent overmodulation (distortion).

How much dynamics processing you should use is a controversial subject. Many listeners think "louder is better," so pop music recordings often have a super-compressed dynamic range (sometimes to the point of destroying dynamics altogether) so they can sound loud. DJs prefer compressed dance music because that minimizes level variations, thus giving more control over level via the DJ mixer's faders. Classical and jazz recordings use little or no compression.

There are several types of dynamics control. Here are the basics for each type.

Manual Gain-Riding

If a track's level is unchanging, then the audio might be too loud during quiet parts, but can be masked by other instruments during loud passages. Before automation, engineers often adjusted the gain manually while mixing and sometimes even when recording—turning down on peaks, turning up during quiet parts—to restrict dynamic range. Although it's difficult to do this quickly and consistently, some engineers still ride gain as a sort of "preliminary compression." And thanks to automation (discussed in Chapter 11), this is a viable technique while mixing.

Level-Riding Plug-Ins

Plug-ins like Waves' Vocal Rider (Fig. 8.1) and Bass Rider do automatic gain riding so that the vocal or bass remains at a target level you specify.

Figure 8.1 Waves' Vocal Rider provides automated gain riding for vocals.

These automatic level-riding plug-ins also write corresponding automation, so you can edit the automation manually if needed. Also, many of these plug-ins offer a *sidechain* input, as described later, to allow controlling the track level based on the overall mix's level—louder in louder passages, and softer in softer passages.

The main advantage of automatic gain-riding programs compared to other dynamics processors is that they don't alter the fidelity or moment-to-moment dynamics, only the overall level. There's no more effect on the signal than you'd have by moving a fader.

As to their effectiveness, for applications where a consistent voice level is crucial—like narration or audio books—vocal gain-riding plug-ins are worth their weight in gold. For music, their usefulness depends on the music itself. These plug-ins can't make artistic decisions, only technical ones. However, gain-riding plug-ins can save a lot of time, and you can edit the automation if you disagree with the levels created by the software.

Normalization

Normalization is a basic type of dynamics control. This process calculates the difference between a recording's highest peak and the maximum available headroom, then amplifies the recording's overall level so that its highest peak reaches a specified level. This is often the maximum level possible short of distortion, but you can usually normalize to a value other than maximum—for example, –2 dB below maximum (see Fig. 8.2).

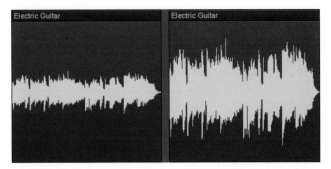

Figure 8.2 The signal on the left hasn't been normalized; its highest peak reaches around –10 dB. The copy on the right has been normalized so that its peak reaches –2 dB.

Limiter

A limiter is like a motor's governor: Signals don't exceed a user-settable threshold. Limiting leaves signals below the threshold untouched, making it a useful processor for digital recording because you don't want signals to exceed 0 dB. By setting the threshold to a level slightly below 0 (like –1 dB), within reason, using a limiter can ensure that distortion doesn't happen (Fig. 8.3).

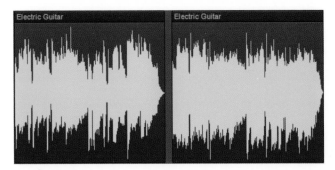

Figure 8.3 The signal on the left hasn't been limited. The copy on the right has been limited by about 6 dB. The peaks have been reduced, which allows for a higher average level (note how the waveform in the limited version is "thicker").

For some audio signals, I prefer limiting over compression (see next) because the limiting effect can be more subtle. However, two cautions apply:

♦ Excessive limiting results in distortion because you can squash a signal only so much before audible artifacts occur.

♦ It's important to choose the proper limiting action. A *brickwall limiter* exerts dictatorial control over level—it gets its name because when the signal hits the threshold, it hits a brick wall. A softer limiting action gives a gentler limiting effect, but may allow overloads to occur.

Limiter Parameters and Controls

Most limiters have fairly basic controls (see Fig. 8.4).

Figure 8.4 This limiter from PreSonus Studio One is representative of limiters in general. The TP switch shows whether intersample distortion is happening (see Chapter 3).

Input

Sending more signal into a limiter causes more of the signal to be limited. Although many limiters have a threshold control to set the amount of limiting, the limiting action with older limiters sometimes depends on increasing the input signal level.

Threshold

This control sets the level above which audio peak limiting occurs.

Ceiling

This control determines the maximum output level. It's like an output level control, except that it gives a precise indication of the level to which the maximum output level will be limited.

Attack

This setting determines how long it takes for limiting to occur after the limiter senses that audio has exceeded the threshold. Higher attack times retain more of a sense of dynamics by letting through initial peaks; however, these peaks will not be subject to limiting and therefore may overload subsequent stages.

Release

Once a signal drops below the threshold, the release control sets how long it takes for limiting to stop, and the signal to become unprocessed. While it might seem you'd want limiting to stop immediately, a signal will often criss-cross the threshold. Going in and out of limiting rapidly may create a buzzy, distorted effect, so adding some release time gives a smoother sound.

Soft Clip

This function not only limits the peaks, but provides a gentle distortion effect. Soft clipping resembles what happens with tape when you send in more signal than the tape can handle.

Gain Reduction Metering

While not a control, gain reduction metering indicates how much the audio is being turned down to keep a signal under the threshold. For example, if the threshold is 0 and the signal is 6 dB above the threshold, then the gain reduction meter will show 6 dB. Higher amounts of gain reduction risk creating artifacts or distortion. Assuming a full-strength input signal, 6 dB of gain reduction is pretty safe; but you can stretch this to 10 dB or even more as needed.

A gain-reduction meter works oppositely from most meters—the *highest* setting is 0, and applying more reduction moves the meter downward from 0 to reflect the reduction amount.

Lookahead

Some limiters delay the audio being processed so they can analyze the real-time signal prior to processing the delayed one. This allows catching an attack as soon as it happens because the limiter anticipates it. The tradeoff is that delaying a track requires delaying the other tracks too so that all the tracks line up in terms of time. Although lookahead increases latency through the system, this may be short enough that the delay is not a problem.

 If latency seems to increase in a project for no apparent reason, you may have inserted a plug-in with lookahead. Most programs will compensate automatically for plug-ins that cause latency, but not all give a warning that this is happening.

How to Adjust the Parameters

Assuming that the limiter sets the amount of limiting with a threshold control and not by adjusting the input level:

1. Start with the input set to unity gain.

2. Reduce the threshold control slowly while observing the gain reduction meter. Listen to how the sound changes as you reduce the threshold.

3. Once the reduction reaches a certain amount, you'll hear artifacts or distortion. Make sure the threshold is considerably above where this happens, while choosing the threshold that gives the desired sound.

4.   Set the release control to auto-release, if available. This will usually give the best results. Otherwise, adjust the release control so it's long enough to avoid a choppy sound, but short enough that there are no noticeable volume variations during the release time.

5.   Similarly, adjust the attack time (if present) to taste.

6.   If limiting causes the output to drop, increase the output level. If the limiter compensates automatically for any reduced output, set the ceiling control for the maximum output—for example, −1 dB to give one dB of headroom.

If you're happy with the sound, move on. However, it's likely you'll re-tweak some of the parameters as the mix develops. When mixing, very few parameters are "set and forget."

Compressor

A compressor evens out variations in dynamic range by amplifying soft signals to make them louder and attenuating loud signals to make them softer. This reduces the difference between soft and loud signals, and increases the sustain of percussive instruments. Although this is similar to limiting, there are differences we need to explore.

Like any dynamics control, compression is not always transparent. Overcompressing gives a pinched, unpleasant sound that can exhibit what engineers call *pumping* and *breathing*. One of the more difficult decisions for beginning engineers is how much to compress, because the ear is not that sensitive to level changes. If you adjust the compressor so you can hear obvious compression effects, it's probably overcompressing.

In most cases, you shouldn't really know a signal is compressed until you bypass the compressor, after which you will note a reduction in punch and apparent level (if not, then you're probably undercompressing). Until you've trained your ears to recognize subtle amounts of compression, keep an eye on the gain reduction meters to avoid overcompressing.

Compression works mainly by lowering a signal's peaks, which allows raising the lower-level signals. For example, suppose some peaks reach to 0, and compression manages to reduce those by −5 dB, so the loudest peaks hit at −5 dB. You can now turn up the signal's overall level by +5 dB, at which point the peaks will once again hit 0. In other words, you've been able to add +5 dB of gain to the overall signal level simply by reducing the peaks.

Unlike a limiter, though, the gain reduction process is more customizable with a compressor—among other features, you can adjust what happens as the audio reaches the threshold for a faster or slower transition into a compressed state, and the rate at which gain reduction occurs.

Compressor Parameters

All compressors have much in common; if you learn one, you're close to learning them all (Fig. 8.5). We'll concentrate on the musical implications of these parameters, and examine how they relate to mixing.

Figure 8.5 Several compressors, clockwise from top: Softube VC 160, Waves V-Comp, Nomad Factory Blue Tubes Compressor FA-770, Universal Audio LA-2A, and Softube VC 76.

Input

Sending more signal into the compressor increases the amount of compression because the audio exceeds the threshold more often. However, unless the compressor uses the input control to set the degree of compression (e.g., the VC 76 referenced in the above picture), you'll usually set the input for unity gain.

The input level influences compressor operation to a great degree because it determines how much signal exceeds the threshold.

Threshold

This sets the level at which compression begins. Above this level, the output increases at a lesser rate than a corresponding input change. Lower thresholds compress more of the signal, so the peaks become lower.

Ratio

This parameter defines how much the output signal changes for a given input signal change (above the threshold). For example, with 2:1 compression, a 2 dB increase at the input yields a 1 dB increase at the output. With 4:1 compression, a 4 dB increase at the input gives a 1 dB increase at the output. Higher ratios increase the effect of compression and tend to sound less natural.

Some compressors provide an "infinite" compression ratio, where the output won't exceed a certain level no matter how much you pump up the input. This is the same function as a limiter.

Attack

A compressor doesn't have to react instantly. The attack control sets how long it takes for the compression to kick in once it senses an input level change. Longer attack times let more of a signal's natural dynamics through, but remember those signals aren't being compressed. Some engineers allow a fair amount of attack time to keep any initial transients intact, but then follow the compressor with a limiter to keep any transients from overloading subsequent stages.

Release

This parameter determines the time required for the compressor to stop affecting the signal once the input passes below the threshold. Longer settings work well with program material because the level changes are more gradual and produce a less noticeable effect. Many compressors also include an auto-release function, which adjusts the release time automatically based on the audio going through the compressor. This usually gives the best results.

Mix

This is not too common a compressor control, but is becoming more popular. In some compressors, the unprocessed and compressed signals are two parallel paths, so this control sets a balance between them. For example, when set halfway, you still get a sense of dynamics from the unprocessed signal, but the compressed signal provides a bigger, more sustained sound.

Knee

This "softens" the compression curve so that the compression ratio increases over time around the threshold, rather than switching instantly at the threshold from no compression to the full compression ratio.

 Don't overlook the knee parameter. A softer knee tends to give a less artificial sound, while a harder knee clamps down harder on the dynamics if needed.

Output Gain and Gain Reduction Meter

After setting the threshold and ratio to squash the peaks, you can use the output (or makeup gain) control to turn the signal's overall level back up again. To help in proper level setting, observe a compressor's gain reduction meter. Like a limiter, the highest setting is 0, and applying more reduction moves the meter downward from 0 to show the amount of reduction. You generally set the output gain control to a little less than the amount of reduction. (For example, if the gain reduction meter shows a maximum of about 5 dB of reduction, around 4 dB is a viable output gain setting.)

Detection Algorithm (Average, Peak, RMS)

This isn't too common an option. The RMS and average settings cause the compressor to react to a signal's average level, whereas the peak setting causes it to react to peak waveform levels. RMS and average response can "beef up" sounds that don't have sharp attacks, including program material, vocals, pads, etc. However, this may still let peaks through. Peak mode works well for controlling transients, which makes it appropriate for percussive sounds where you don't want transients to exceed the available headroom.

Lookahead

This works the same way as with limiters (see previous).

Type

Different compressors use different methods to compress a signal. For example, older units used light-dependent resistors to provide gain control. If the input became louder, it drove a small light bulb that became brighter. This shined on the light-dependent resistor, reduced the resistance, and altered the gain. Some compressors include the option to choose among various compressor technology emulations.

Different compressor technologies can sound quite different. Try the various options on different types of signals to learn their responses.

How to Adjust the Parameters

Assuming, like the limiter, that the compressor sets the amount of limiting with a threshold control and not by adjusting the input level:

1. Start with the input set to unity gain and ratio set to 1.5:1.

2. Reduce the threshold control slowly while observing the gain reduction meter. The greater the amount of gain reduction, the more you'll hear the effects of compression.

3. Adjust the ratio control, if needed. The threshold and ratio controls interact. Threshold increases the amount of overall compression, while ratio makes the compression effect more drastic. Over time, you'll learn through experience which control requires adjustment for the desired effect.

4. Past a certain amount of gain reduction, the compression will sound like an effect. This may or may not be what you want. Adjust the threshold accordingly.

5. If the action is too drastic, change the knee to a gentler compression curve.

6. Set the release and attack controls similarly to how they're set for a limiter (see previous).

7. Increase the output level to compensate for the level loss caused by introducing compression. There may be an auto-gain control that compensates automatically for any volume drop.

Parameter Adjustment Tips

Compression is deceptively difficult to set up correctly, so here are some tips.

♦ **Start with a conservative gain-reduction setting.** Unless you want an obviously compressed sound, you usually don't want more than 6 dB of gain reduction. To reduce the amount of gain reduction, either raise the threshold or reduce the ratio.

♦ **Vocals get along well with compression.** Compression brings up low-level sounds, so vocals can sound more "human" because you hear mouth noises, breaths, and other elements that add expressiveness. It's not uncommon for compression on vocals to use a much higher compression ratio, and lower threshold, than other instruments.

♦ **For a more natural sound, use lower compression ratios (1.5:1 to 3:1).** Bass typically uses a ratio of around 3:1, voice 2:1 to 6:1—but these are approximations, not rules. To increase sustain of an instrument like guitar, try a ratio in the 4:1 to 8:1 range.

♦ **Attack time settings.** A minimum attack time clamps peaks almost instantly, which can sound unnatural. If it's crucial that the signal never hit 0, yet you want really high average levels, try using a limiter.

For most sounds, an attack time of 3 to10 ms lets through some peaks for a more natural effect, although you'll need to lower the output level so the peaks don't distort subsequent stages. If this is a problem, follow the compressor with a limiter set for a high threshold so all it does is catch transients.

♦ **Release time is not as critical as attack time.** Start with release in the 100 to 250 ms range. Shorter times sound livelier; longer times sound smoother. However, too short a release time can give a choppy effect, while too long a release time homogenizes the sound.

♦ **Auto release settings are good.** Use these, especially if you're new to compression.

♦ **Reality checks are important.** Toggle the bypass switch frequently to compare the compressed and non-compressed sounds. Match levels closely for the most realistic comparison. Even a little compression may give the desired effect.

♦ **Place compression early in the signal chain.** When using compression as a track effect, place it early in any signal processing chain so it doesn't bring up noise from preceding effects.

♦ **Compressor/limiters are not miracle workers.** No compressor can compensate for dead strings or guitars with poor sustain characteristics.

♦ **Add compression before distortion for sustain.** This gives a smoother sound, and doesn't bring up noise from the distortion.

♦ **Check your input levels.** If you experience a sudden increase in compression, but you didn't increase the compression amount, the input signal going to the compressor may have increased.

Multiband Compressor

With a traditional compressor, a signal that exceeds the threshold reduces the gain and affects all frequencies—if a strong kick drum hits above the threshold, it will also reduce the level of the cymbals and other high-frequency sounds. Multiband compressors split an incoming signal into several bands, like a graphic equalizer. Each band has a compressor, so compression affects only the specific frequency band it's associated with (Fig. 8.6).

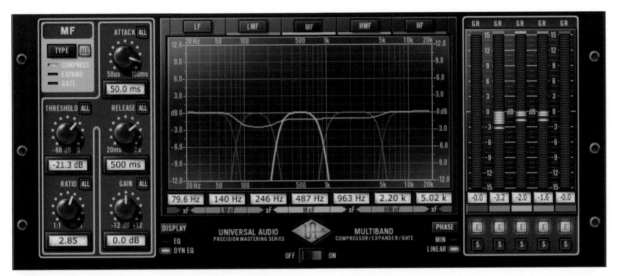

Figure 8.6 The different-colored "domes" on the graph are particular frequency ranges; the blue line toward the center shows the composite result of the compression in the various bands. The meters on the right indicate the amount of gain reduction being applied.

With multiband compression, if the kick drum is in a low-frequency band, and the high-hats and cymbals are in a high-frequency band, you can compress the kick drum without affecting the high-hats and cymbals. This gives more transparent dynamics control than single-band compressors.

 A multiband compressor can serve as a high-performance graphic equalizer if you set the ratio for all bands to no compression (1.0 or 1:1), albeit with fewer bands than typical graphic equalizers.

Multiband Compressor Controls

Each band's compressor has standard compressor controls. The only major differences may be ways to adjust the same control on all bands simultaneously, and a solo and/or mute button for each band so you can hear how compression affects one or more particular bands.

Each band will also have a level control, which means a multiband compressor combines some of the characteristics of a graphic equalizer. In the previous example using drums, if you didn't want to compress the high-hats and cymbals but have them be more prominent in the mix, you could simply raise the level a bit in the high-frequency band where the cymbals live.

Multiband compression is useful with complex program material, like a two-track mix. Although multiband compressors are popular for mastering, don't overlook what they can do with individual tracks, particularly ones that cover a wide frequency range (like drums).

Applying Multiband Compression

For a hotter, louder sound, set the compressor parameters similarly for each band. In this case, the multiband compressor acts like a standard compressor, but gives a more transparent sound because of the multiple bands.

For adjusting individual bands, consider the following tips:

♦ Because most multiband compressors have level controls for each band, you can initially treat the device like a graphic EQ. If turning up a band improves the sound, that may indicate the need for some compression. If turning a band down helps, consider not compressing it, and instead adjust the level for the best effect.

♦ Next, adjust the compression ratio settings. This can be tricky because changes you make in one band often affect how you perceive the other bands. For example, if you compress the midrange, the treble and bass may appear weaker.

♦ Avoid exceeding a 1.5:1 or 2:1 compression ratio at first, and keep the threshold relatively high, such as −3 to −9 dB. This will tame the highest peaks, without affecting too much else of the signal. Listen after each change, and allow your ears to acclimate to the sound before making additional changes. If your multiband compressor can save presets, save them periodically as temp 1, temp 2, temp 3, etc. That way you can return to a previous, less radical setting if you lose your way.

♦ First, work on any bands with problems. Once they sound right, tweak the other bands to work well with the changes you've made.

Loudness Maximizer

This specialized type of limiter (usually with a multiband design) establishes a strict dynamic range ceiling. However, because maximizers are designed to put as much level as possible on a master recording, they operate somewhat differently than standard limiters because they need to give extreme amounts of limiting while still sounding relatively natural. The controls for each band are similar to those for limiters (Fig. 8.7).

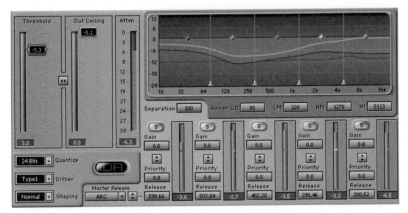

Figure 8.7   The Waves L3 Multimaximizer provides a great degree of control and sounds surprisingly transparent.

With individual instruments, maximizers work well to bring out a solo: select the region containing the solo, then apply a couple dB of maximization (don't add too much). This will lift the solo out of the mix compared to other sections. For individual instruments, maximization generally goes last in the signal chain, except with time-delay effects. Processing these effects' tails can sound unnatural.

Expander

An expander is the opposite of a compressor, yet has similar controls. Below a threshold, the output drops off *faster* than the input. For example with an expansion ratio of 1:2, lowering an input level that is below the threshold by 1 dB lowers the output level by 2 dB. You can consider an expander a more refined version of a noise gate (discussed later in this chapter).

You'll often find processors that combine expansion and gating (Fig. 8.8), much like how compressors may also include limiting.

Figure 8.8   The Nomad Factory Blue Tubes Gate Expander GX622 has the standard expander and gate controls, but also has an internal sidechain that triggers the gate only for audio within a specific frequency range. The Listen button lets you hear the effect of the high-pass and low-pass filters on the sidechain audio.

The expander's most common application is reducing residual, low-level noise. This uses a low threshold (around –45 to –60 dB) with a steep expansion ratio, like 1:4 or 1:10. The reduction may sound natural enough to eliminate the need for manual editing. Expansion can be effective to reduce hiss between vocal phrases, amp noise between guitar licks, and the like. Expanders can also provide special effects, like speeding up an instrument's natural decay.

Transient Shaper

A transient shaper is a specialized dynamics processor that affects a signal's attack; it can either emphasize or soften the initial transient. However, unlike a compressor or limiter, this doesn't necessarily change the overall signal level. There's typically a single, rotary control where the center position does nothing, rotating clockwise sharpens the attack by amplifying it, and rotating counter-clockwise softens the attack by ramping up more slowly. Some transient shapers also include a sustain control that brings up the average level after the initial decay (called Weight in the following screenshot). The result is somewhat like a compressor that separates the initial attack and sustain elements (Fig. 8.9).

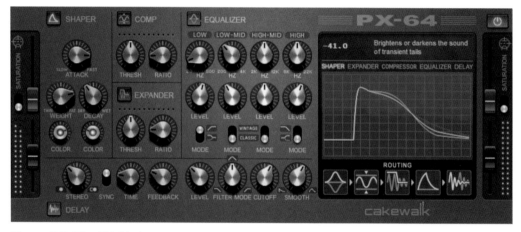

Figure 8.9 The PX-64 drum processor includes a transient shaper (left) with sustain, as well as a Weight control to make the decay thinner or fatter, and Color controls that emphasize or de-emphasize the Weight and Decay controls' frequency response.

Multiband transient shapers, like Waves' Trans-X, are particularly useful with drum loops or mixes because they can shape the attack of low frequency sounds (like kick) independently of midrange and high-frequency instruments.

Two cautions apply with transient shapers:

♦ Unless there's a smooth transition from the attack to the post-attack sound, the two can sound separated. You can usually fix this with proper control adjustments.

♦ Emphasizing the attack can exceed the available headroom. Native Instruments' Transient Master (Fig. 8.10) includes a limiter to help with this, but not all transient shapers do.

Figure 8.10   The Transient Master processor from Native Instruments' Komplete software suite is designed for making quick adjustments when mixing. The Attack control handles the initial transients. Sustain affects the sound's body.

Transient shaping has many uses for mixing. It can:

♦ Emphasize drum and other percussive attacks so they stand out in the mix without increasing level.

♦ Reduce the attack of overly aggressive drums. For example, reducing tom attacks can place them more behind the kick and snare.

♦ Soften the attack of steel-string acoustic guitars if the attack overshadows the guitar sound itself.

♦ Reduce the attack on electric guitars prior to an amp sim. This reduces the non-tonal "splash" of pick noise that often produces a harsh-sounding initial transient.

♦ Lower a signal's sustain to reduce room sound or reverb effects.

♦ Increase attack and reduce sustain to bring a sound more to the mix's forefront, or soften the attack to place an instrument more in the background.

♦ Increase sustain to make sounds seem bigger.

♦ Emphasize the attack of a bass to give more punch. Increasing the sustain gives a fatter, more even sound.

Noise Gate

A noise gate silences the track's audio when the level drops below a user-settable threshold and passes the audio through when the level returns above the threshold. The original use for noise gates was to reduce tape hiss. By setting the threshold just above the noise level, a track would be silenced while there was no program material. As soon as a signal occurred that was louder than the hiss, the gate would open and allow the signal through.

Noise gates are most effective on signals without much noise because you can set the threshold low enough that the gating action doesn't impact what you *want* to hear. For example, a noise gate can help remove mic preamp hiss between vocal phrases. Noise gates can also provide effects, such as:

♦ Cutting off the ring from sustaining drum sounds, like toms.

♦ Removing the room ambiance "tail" from percussive instruments.

♦ Shortening reverb decay times.

♦ Reducing leakage—for example if a snare track has leakage from other drums, it may be possible to reduce the leakage by setting the threshold above the leakage but below the snare.

♦ Cutting off the decay of percussive sounds so only the peaks play through, which makes the sound more percussive.

Because the raw gating action can sound unnatural, the typical noise gate has controls to make the gating transitions less abrupt (see Fig. 8.11).

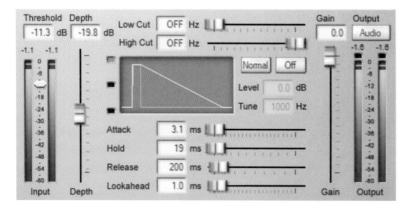

Figure 8.11 A typical noise gate offers several ways to modify the gate's action and make it less obtrusive.

Noise Gate Parameters

Noise gate parameters have much in common with other dynamics processor parameters.

Threshold

This control sets the level where the gate opens and closes. Some noise gates have separate threshold controls for gate on and gate off so that a loud attack is required to turn the gate on, while a lower threshold must be reached during the decay before the gate turns off.

Attack

This control sets the time between when the noise gate detects a signal above the threshold and when the gate actually opens. Here are some applications where an attack time is desirable:

♦ If you are getting a click when the gate opens, a short attack time (0.1 to 2 ms) can reduce or eliminate the clicks.

♦ Adding an attack time softens an instrument's attack so it's not as prominent.

♦ An attack time around 100 ms causes a signal to "swell" to its maximum level. For instance, if the performance pauses briefly between notes, when a new note exceeds the threshold it will fade in over the specified attack time. This alters the attack characteristics of percussive instruments like piano and guitar, and adds "brass-like" attacks to sustained sounds.

   However, this requires a space before every note that needs an attack so that the gate can reset itself. Also note that any Release and Hold parameters (see next) should be set at minimum. Otherwise, the gate may remain open during the space between notes, which prevents triggering a new attack when a new note plays. Conversely, too short a release can result in a "chattering" effect. Use the shortest possible decay time consistent with a smooth sound.

♦ Attack time can reduce vocal breath inhales. A singer breathing in can trigger the gate. As the inhale fades in, so does the gate. This makes the breath sound less prominent, but doesn't cut it out completely (which can sound unnatural).

Release (or Decay)

After a signal drops below the threshold, the decay time ramps the level down over the specified time to provide a smooth transition from the gate being open to closed. A typical decay value is 200 ms.

Hold

This complements the Attack and Release controls. After a signal goes below the threshold, Hold keeps the gate open for a certain amount of time before the release time starts. This is useful for signals with long, slow decays (e.g., long reverb tails) where the signal crosses over the threshold several times as it fades, which can produce a "chattering" effect. Increasing the hold time lets the gate stay open if it drops briefly below the threshold. Once the signal drops below the threshold for good, the release phase begins after the hold time elapses.

Attenuation or Range

Instead of muting the audio completely when the gate closes, it's usually possible to attenuate the audio by a certain amount so the transition doesn't go to full silence. Try an attenuation setting around 10 dB. This cuts most of the noise, and may sound more natural because when the gate turns off, there's a less abrupt transition. At a maximum attenuation setting, no sound will get through the gate.

Lookahead

Some noise gates offer a lookahead function. This delays the audio going through the gate, allowing the gate to analyze the incoming, non-delayed signal. The gate can then anticipate when a transient will occur, and open just before the transient hits to prevent cutting off the transient's beginning.

Gate Mode

Some gates provide two standard options—normal and duck. We've already discussed normal gate operation. Ducking reverses the gate's action so that stronger signals close the gate. The gate then returns to its open position according to the Hold and Release times. The most common use for ducking is with sidechaining (see next).

 With sidechaining, ducking can reduce one signal in response to another signal (e.g., reduce background music when dialog occurs).

Sidechaining

Usually, the input signal entering a processor determines the amount of compression, gating, etc.—in other words, the input is the signal that's either above or below the threshold, and causes the processor to react in a certain way. However, some compressors, noise gates, limiters, and other processors include a feature called *sidechaining*. This separates the audio signal going into the processor from the audio signal that controls the dynamics. The latter becomes the sidechain input (see Fig. 8.12).

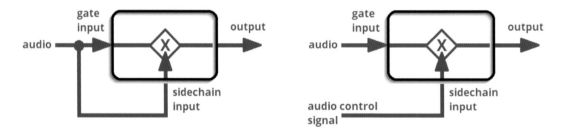

Figure 8.12 The block diagram on the left shows how the input signal controls a noise gate, while the diagram on the right shows the noise gate being controlled by a separate sidechain input.

Probably the best way to explain this is with a couple examples:

♦ Assume you're mixing a singer-songwriter project with vocal and guitar, and the guitar goes through a compressor. You can split the vocal into two paths, and send one to the compressor's sidechain input. A vocal level above the threshold will compress the guitar, making it quieter during vocal passages. When the singer isn't singing, the guitar will return to its uncompressed state.

♦ Suppose you have a noise gate with sidechaining on a bass guitar track. You can feed the kick drum into the sidechain input. The gate on the bass guitar will open when the kick drum hit is above the threshold and close when the kick drum hit drops below the threshold. This creates a super-tight rhythm section.

 Sidechaining with compression is used a lot in EDM productions to obtain "pumping" sounds by triggering compression with the kick or snare.

Should Compression Go Before or After EQ?

There's no universal answer to this question, because compression can serve different purposes. Both options (before and after EQ) have their uses.

Consider this scenario: You've recorded a great synth bass line with a highly resonant filter sweep. On some notes, the level goes too high when a note's frequency coincides with the filter frequency. Otherwise, the signal is well behaved. But, you also want to boost the lower midrange a bit to give a beefier sound.

Put the compressor first to trap those rogue transients, then apply EQ to the more dynamically consistent sound. Because the EQ change is minor, it won't change the signal's overall amplitude much.

Now suppose you don't have any problems with overly resonant filters, but you do need a massive lower midrange boost. This much boost could greatly increase the amplitude at some frequencies, so putting compression after the EQ will help even these out a bit.

However, there's a complication. Because significant boosts in a certain frequency range increase level in that range, the compressor will scale those levels back down a bit. So this reduces the effect of what the EQ is trying to do—it tries to boost, but the compressor won't let it go much further. However, signals below the threshold *do* remain boosted, and this might give the sound you want.

Another reason to place EQ before compression is to make the compression more frequency-sensitive. To emphasize a guitar part's melody, boost EQ slightly for the range to be emphasized and then compress. The boosted frequencies will cross over the compression threshold sooner than the other frequencies.

Or, suppose a digital synth is "buzzy." Cut the highs a bit prior to compression, and the compressor will bring up everything else more readily than the highs. This type of technique isn't quite the same as multiband compression, but gives some of the same results because there's more punch to the boosted frequencies.

Key Takeaways

♦ Although dynamics processing was originally designed to solve problems—and it still does—it's also used as a creative special effect.

♦ The most basic form of dynamics processing is an engineer changing a fader or level control manually, like reducing gain when recording a band that starts playing louder.

♦ Plug-ins are available that ride levels on playback to maintain a consistent volume. Unlike other types of dynamics control, this doesn't alter the audio's dynamic range, only its dynamics.

♦ Normalization calculates the difference between a recording's highest peak and the maximum available headroom, then amplifies the recording's overall level so that its highest peak reaches a specified level.

♦ A limiter is like a motor's governor: Signals are restricted so they don't exceed a user-settable threshold.

♦ A compressor evens out variations in dynamic range by amplifying soft signals to make them louder, and attenuating loud signals to make them softer.

♦ Lookahead allows a dynamics processor to analyze a signal before processing, which gives greater accuracy. The tradeoff is that this adds delay (latency) to the signal.

♦ Multiband compressors split an incoming signal into several bands, like a graphic equalizer. Each band has a compressor, so compression affects only its associated band.

♦ A maximizer is a specialized type of limiter (usually with a multiband design) that applies extreme amounts of limiting while still sounding relatively natural.

♦ An expander is the opposite of a compressor: below a threshold, a level decrease at the input becomes a much greater level decrease at the output.

♦ A transient shaper is a specialized dynamics processor that affects a signal's attack. It can either emphasize or soften the initial transient.

♦ Noise gates mute the track's audio when the level drops below a user-settable threshold, and unmutes the audio when the level returns above the threshold.

♦ Sidechaining separates the audio signal going into the processor from the audio signal that controls the dynamics, so that one audio signal can control the dynamics of a different audio signal.

♦ There's no universal answer as to whether compression should go before or after equalization, because compression can serve different purposes. Both options have their uses.

Chapter 9

Adding Other Effects

Although equalization and dynamics control are important, many other processors can enhance a mix. Thousands of plug-ins all claim to do wonderful things, and they often can enhance a track. However, it's important not to get carried away, particularly because there are many free plug-ins—and you don't *need* 46 compressors. Really.

One of my favorite plug-in stories involves *Sound on Sound* magazine's Mix Rescue series, where the magazine's editors go to someone's studio and show how to improve a mix. During one of these, the musician who owned the studio went into the kitchen to make tea. Meanwhile, the *Sound on Sound* people bypassed all the plug-ins so they could hear what the raw tracks sounded like. When the musician returned, he wanted to know what they had done to make the sound *so* much better.

Often a raw track doesn't need much more than EQ or dynamics, if that. Piling more processing on a track can create a more artificial sound. Remember too that a song's tracks work *together*. When adding effects, do so in context. If all the tracks are gussied up with plug-ins to sound fantastic, the end result will likely be a confusing mess. Think of effects as spices for cooking: Too much of a good thing can be a bad thing. Also, avoid using an effect in an attempt to salvage a part. If a part has problems, re-do it rather than try to cover up the flaws with effects.

However, there are situations when adding the right plug-in at the right time can lift a song to a higher level. Let's take a look at some popular plug-ins used for mixing.

Console Emulation

Before digital audio, mixing used analog consoles. This technology has several differences compared to digital mixing, and certain mixing consoles were known for particular sonic characters. They were essentially subtle signal processors, and some people considered that sound desirable. Today we have plug-ins that emulate the sound of specific consoles to provide analog character in our digital world.

Several console emulators, such as Waves' NLS Non-Linear Summer plug-ins, the console emulators in Cakewalk by BandLab, and Slate Digital's Virtual Console Collection, include separate emulation plug-ins for console channels and busses. (Fig. 9.1).

Figure 9.1 Console emulation models are often different for channels and busses, as with Slate Digital's VCC (Virtual Console Collection).

Console Emulation Basics

Three main considerations cause analog consoles to sound different compared to mixing in the box:

♦ Analog circuitry has inherent non-linearities (or in less polite terms, distortion). As a signal goes through multiple analog stages, these non-linearities add up and create a subtle change. When distortion generates harmonics in the audio spectrum's upper range, the "soundstage" may appear wider because highs are more directional. This can also produce a mild form of the "sparkle" associated with processors like exciters.

♦ Consoles often used audio transformers to match signal levels and impedances. Transformers are some of the most complex signal processors in any signal chain, and their characteristics depend on the circuitry that surrounds them—for example, the external circuitry may dampen some of the "ringing" that occurs when passing square waves through an audio transformer. Transformers also generate distortion that's highest at lower frequencies.

♦ There may be *crosstalk,* where low-level signals leak into adjacent channels. Some engineers feel this helps "glue" the sound together.

I once visited composer Wendy Carlos when she had an Akai MG1212 digital tape recorder, and it sounded much better than other MG1212 machines I'd heard. She had simply added transformers to the inputs and outputs, and that's when I realized how important transformers could be to the sound. Transformer emulations provide a somewhat fatter low end with added warmth.

To underscore the sonic variety of analog consoles, some console emulators create subtle, random differences among channels. Waves' NLS Non-Linear Summer plug-ins take an unusual approach by modeling multiple channels from the same console rather than a single idealized channel. This is intended to provide more of an analog console's feel.

Inserting Console Emulation Plug-Ins

With console emulation isolated on an individual channel, you might not hear a significant difference. However, adding console emulation to every channel and bus has a cumulative effect. Prior to mixing, I often insert a console emulator plug-in as the last effect in a channel or bus's chain of effects. (This is a personal preference—some people put the console emulator first in an effects chain, others place console emulation only on selected channels). To make it easier to handle multiple console emulator instances, some console emulators include grouping functions. Unlike traditional mixer groups these aren't about routing, but allow controlling multiple console emulators from a centralized location (Fig. 9.2).

Figure 9.2 Waves' NLS console emulation package includes a VCA Groups Console area for controlling emulators within the console that are assigned to specific groups. For example if all the drum channels are assigned to Group 1, then you can adjust the Group 1 Drive and Trim controls for all drum channels simultaneously.

The reason for inserting console emulation before you begin mixing is that you can't necessarily predict how console emulation will affect the sound, so you'll want to make your EQ and dynamics decisions with those changes already in place—just as if you were mixing on an analog mixer. If you wait until later in the mixing process, then you may have to go back and compensate for the difference.

Tech Talk: Testing Console Emulations

Although the effects are subtle, console emulators do create measurable differences. I generated sine waves at various frequencies, and then processed them through three console emulations included in Cakewalk by BandLab to see how they and their controls affected the sound (Fig. 9.3).

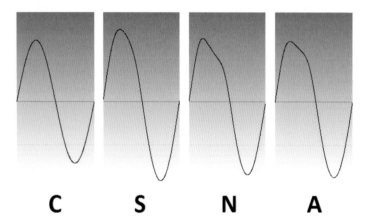

C   S   N   A

Figure 9.3 The non-processed, "control" sine wave is at the left. The waveforms for Cakewalk's three different emulations (S-Type, N-Type, and A-Type) are to the right.

To run tests of your own, you can use MAGIX Sound Forge, Steinberg WaveLab, or Adobe Audition to generate high-quality sine waves (you can also download sampled sine waves from the net). You'll learn a lot when you hear how the console emulation controls affect the sound.

Of course, you wouldn't judge a console emulator by how it processes sine waves, but testing at various frequencies provides an understanding of how the controls affect particular frequency ranges.

Console Channel Strips

In addition to console emulation, many companies offer emulations of particular console channel strips. Some of the most iconic channel strips are incorporated in Universal Audio's plug-ins, IK Multimedia's T-RackS software suite, Softube Console 1 controller (Fig. 9.4), and the Waves SSL 4000.

Figure 9.4 Softube's Console 1 models the SSL 4000 E mixer channel strip, but pairs this with a hardware controller for adjusting the EQ, dynamics, and analog console saturation.

Although these plug-ins aren't considered console emulators per se, they do emulate the element that contributed much to a console's particular sound.

Can You *Really* Hear a Difference?

One aspect that makes console emulation enigmatic is that it's not a broadband effect. It affects different frequencies differently, particularly with respect to transformer emulations and varying input levels. Some people hear a major difference in their mixes, while others feel it's no big deal.

When I first started using console emulation, I wasn't impressed. But as I learned how to tame it and mix "through" it, I began using it more and more. Sometimes the results *are* subtle, but if the end result is better than not using it, that's what matters.

Tape Emulation

Tape is also a signal processor—people don't like the sound of tape for its accuracy, but rather for its *inaccuracies.* Send a sine wave oscillator into a tape track and increase the level slowly: audible distortion can start with signals as low as –20 dB, and distortion increases as the level increases. However, unlike digital distortion, many people subjectively perceive this type of distortion as pleasing—hence tape emulation plug-ins. Also, by reducing the higher peaks and opening up headroom, tape emulation allows for higher average levels than undistorted signals.

Tape machines had adjustments for trading off noise, distortion, and frequency response, as well as ways to change tape speed (different speeds alter both high-frequency response and where a low-frequency response peak occurs). Some plug-ins include these adjustments so you can tailor the tape sound even further. There are plenty of tape emulation plug-ins, and some host software includes tape saturation effects (Fig. 9.5).

Figure 9.5 Cakewalk by BandLab includes a tape emulation plug-in.

There are also hardware options, like the Rupert Neve Designs 542 Tape Emulator (Fig. 9.6).

Figure 9.6 The Rupert Neve 542 packages the tape emulation from their Portico 5042 into a 500-series module. It models a tape machine's electronics as well as what the tape itself does.

Where to Insert Tape Emulation Plug-Ins

Here again, there are no rules. Tape emulation can enhance some instruments, but not others. For example, I don't use it with vocals, tambourines, or other percussion instruments with lots of high-frequency energy. However, acoustic guitar can sound fuller with tape distortion, due to the higher average level from reducing attack transients, along with some slight distortion sparkle. Tape also provides "limiting with character" for drums, and the inherent bass boost that happens with the 7.5 and 15 IPS (inches per second) settings can add depth to electric and synth bass.

You likely won't want tape emulation on every channel (although you might for a "vintage" sound). The most realistic tape emulation placement is first in any chain of effects because in a tape-based studio, the signal coming from tape would feed into the mixer.

Distortion

Although one of the goals of audio engineering is to rid audio systems of distortion, there are creative ways to use distortion—and several ways to add distortion with plug-ins.

Saturation

Saturation refers to processors that distort signals. There are three main saturation categories:

♦ Tube saturation

♦ Tape saturation (part of tape emulation plug-ins)

♦ General saturation that may be based on hardware, but isn't necessarily a strict emulation of a particular product or technology (or may combine multiple saturation types in a single plug-in)

Tube Saturation

The Wave Arts TS-2 tube saturator, which emulates a 12AX7 or 12AU7 tube, is optimized specifically for tube-type saturation. It also includes equalization (Fig. 9.7).

Figure 9.7 The Wave Arts TS-2 tube saturator provides a precise tube model. The company also offers the similar but older Tube Saturator Vintage plug-in for free. However, it requires far more CPU power than the TS-2.

Plug-ins that emulate tube-based gear inherently provide tube emulation. Overloading these provides effects similar to overloading tubes. (Fig. 9.8).

Figure 9.8 The Tube-Tech PE 1C and ME 1B equalizers emulate the characteristics of the tubes inside the original hardware units.

Amp Simulators

There's a romanticism around tube distortion because of guitar amps, but what makes the *total* amp sound is a combination of tubes, transformers, and most importantly, the speaker and cabinet; by itself, an overloaded tube doesn't sound all that wonderful. Amp sims, like Native Instruments' Guitar Rig and IK Multimedia's AmpliTube (Fig. 9.9), include tube saturation and the other elements that contribute to a guitarist's sound.

Figure 9.9 IK Multimedia's AmpliTube models the tube preamp stage, power amp, speaker cabinet, and effects associated with a variety of guitar amps. This view shows cabinet and mic modeling, as well as virtual mic placement.

An amp sim's usefulness extends beyond guitar and bass. For example, if you want a variety of different tube distortions, bypass everything except for an amp's preamp module. Some of these are cleaner than others, some more distorted, some have tone controls, etc. An amp sim can sometimes be the fastest and most versatile way to add a tube sound to tracks.

General Saturation

Some plug-ins provide one-stop shopping for saturation. PSP's MixSaturator2 has three different saturation sections: one for bass frequencies that adds harmonics and simulates the head bump found in tape that increases low frequency response, one with a treble processing algorithm that simulates tape saturation without increasing the overall distortion, and one providing an overall saturation algorithm with seven different emulations (including tube distortion, tape, and digital clipping; see Fig. 9.10).

Figure 9.10 PSP's MixSaturator2 is part of their MixPack2 bundle—a plug-in suite designed specifically for mixing.

Other plug-ins combine saturation with other modules. For example Universal Audio's SPL TwinTube models the SPL hardware product that follows tube saturation with a tube-based harmonics processor to add sparkle (Fig. 9.11).

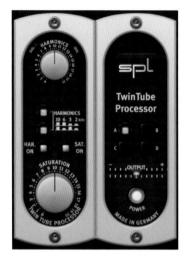

Figure 9.11 Universal Audio's SPL TwinTube is a software version of the SPL TwinTube hardware.

Applying Saturation

Distortion on guitar is the sound of rock and roll, but saturation is useful for more than guitar. Also remember, you can use external hardware, including distortion-specific guitar processors, with your host software (see Chapter 4). Here are some applications for distortion that don't involve guitar.

Drums. Drums have a quick initial attack, followed by an abrupt decay. Adding a little distortion clips the attack's first few milliseconds, while leaving the decay untouched. This affects the sound in three important ways:

♦ You can raise the drum's overall average level for a louder perceived sound because the overdrive effect acts like a primitive limiter.

♦ Clipping creates a short period of time where the sound is at its maximum level, which contributes a feeling of "punch."

♦ Distortion increases the attack's harmonic content, producing a brighter attack.

Moderate distortion can "toughen up" drums, particularly analog electronic drums—adding a little distortion to vintage drum machines can turn them from audio wimps into turbulent filth monsters. Kick drums are candidates for significant amounts of distortion. However, be sparing with cymbals and high-hats, which often sound harsh with distortion. Parallel processing is useful because it combines a distorted signal path with the natural drum sounds.

Another option is to use saturation as a send effect, which is particularly applicable to electronic and virtual drums with multiple outputs (e.g., distort the kick and snare, but not the hi-hat and cymbals). Even a little distortion can add a great edge to drums, including acoustic drums and percussion loops.

Softube's free Saturation Knob plug-in is useful for drums because the three Saturation Type positions allow saturating different frequency ranges (Fig. 9.12).

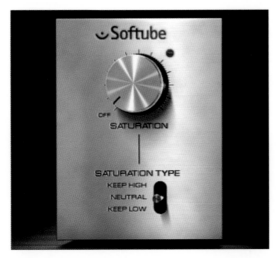

Figure 9.12 Softube's Saturation Knob offers three ways to tailor the saturation to specific frequency ranges.

Bass. Adding saturation to bass tracks is one of my favorite mixing tricks. The bass stands out in the mix more because the extra "grit" adds very audible high frequencies. Also, saturation acts like a limiter because it cuts off the peaks, which opens up headroom so you can increase the overall level. However, with amp sim distortion, consider patching the distortion in parallel with the bass track to retain the low end's fullness. Bass seems to sound best with relatively low-gain distortion settings because this gives more of a deep, aggressive growl that cuts well through a mix. Too much distortion can compete with the guitar sound.

Vocals. Hardcore/industrial groups sometimes add distortion to vocals for a dirty, disturbing effect.

Keyboards. Classic tonewheel organ sounds often took advantage of overdriving a rotating speaker's preamp to create distortion. Adding saturation to synthesized organ sounds can give extra character-building dirt. Keep the gain fairly low; you don't want a fizzy sound. Like bass and drums, parallel processing usually gives the best results.

Aux bus/send effects distortion. To bring just a couple instruments out from a mix, patch a distortion plug-in set for very little distortion into an aux bus during mixdown. Turn up the aux send for individual channels to make them jump out.

Where to Insert EQ with Distortion

"Clean" effects that follow distortion can make the distortion sound smoother. The classic example is reverb. Adding some really gorgeous room ambiance to a distorted signal takes off some of the edge. But placing distortion *after* reverb will distort the reverb tails, which sounds unrealistic as well as dirty.

The same is true for discrete echoes (delay): echo a distorted sound; don't distort an echoed sound. With lots of delay feedback, the distorted echoes will eventually degenerate into a distorted mess. If the echo is post-distortion, then the echoes remain distinct.

One possible exception is EQ. You usually want EQ after distortion, so it can alter the distorted sound's timbre. But just as you can use EQ before compression to give a more "frequency-sensitive" effect, EQ before distortion causes certain frequency ranges to distort more readily than others. For example, if you boost a synth's midrange to distort sooner than the bass, the melody gets chunky but the bass doesn't. I often add EQ both before and after distortion—the first to alter what gets distorted, and the second to alter the distorted sound itself.

Delay

Adding delay to tracks has been popular since slapback echo from a tape recorder graced rockabilly rhythm guitar and vocals. Even subtle amounts of delay can help fill out a sound, particularly vocals.

Delay Parameters

There are three main parameters associated with delay effects.

Delay Time

This setting determines the amount of time between the input signal and the first echo. With multiple successive echoes, delay time also represents the time difference between subsequent echoes. You'll be able to dial in a specific delay time, like 300 milliseconds; modern delay plug-ins also often include an option to sync the delay time to your host program's tempo (Fig. 9.13).

Figure 9.13 Most delay plug-ins can synchronize echo time to the host's tempo. In this example the Sync switch is on, and the Echo Delay readout shows 1/8 note.

Older hardware delay units may not have sync to tempo, but you can calculate the amount of delay for specific tempos. Use the formula **60,000/tempo in BPM = quarter-note delay time in milliseconds**. For example, for a quarter-note delay at 95 BPM, set the delay time to 60,000/95 = 631.6 milliseconds.

 An eighth-note delay is good for thickening vocals. Mix the echo level fairly low—just enough to reinforce the vocal.

Feedback

Also called *recirculation*, the feedback control allows you to create multiple echoes by feeding the output back into the input. When the echo re-enters the input, it's delayed again, which creates another echo.

If you include EQ in the feedback path, the timbre of successive echoes will change over time. For example, if the feedback path reduces the high frequencies, then each successive echo will sound less bright than the previous one.

Mix

This sets the balance of echoes with the original, unprocessed signal. When inserting echo in an aux bus, you will usually want the Mix set to 100% of the processed (wet) sound because the main channel fader will provide the unprocessed (dry) sound.

Other Delay Features

Like everything else in the world of recording, manufacturers are always trying to come up with interesting new features. Here are some common ones.

Tapped Delay

This type of plug-in has multiple delays, each with independent delay times, mix, feedback, panning, and so on, for setting up complex delay patterns (including polyrhythmic delay effects). The PSP 608 MultiDelay is one of my favorites (Fig. 9.14).

Figure 9.14 The PSP 608 MultiDelay offers eight taps, each with filtering, stereo imaging, modulation, saturation, and other controls for extreme flexibility. This preset provides the basis for modeling a room sound.

Delay Mode

This determines echo placement in the stereo field. In ping-pong mode, successive echoes alternate between the left and right channels. In LCR mode, successive echoes route to the left, center, and right before repeating the pattern. There may also be an RCL mode for repeating in the right, center, and left channels.

Modulation

Modulation causes slight delay time variations, which adds an effect somewhat like electronic chorusing. This is often useful with guitar and keyboards.

 Modulation usually varies delay as a percentage of the total delay time. So a little bit of modulation at shorter delays can create a huge variation with longer delays.

Tape Echo Emulation

Tape echo, being mechanical, was imperfect—there were slight speed flutters, and if the tape heads weren't maintained, the high frequency response would suffer. Tape also tended to boost low frequencies and add hiss. Delay plug-ins may emulate these effects.

Equalization

In addition to EQ in the feedback path, EQ in general can be useful with echo. If no EQ is included in the plug-in itself, you can insert echo in a send, insert a filter in the send after or before the echo, set the echo for delayed sound only, and then mix in the desired amount of filtered echo with the main signal (see Fig. 9.15).

Rolling off the lows either going into the delay or coming out of it will help prevent the echo effect from muddying the lower midrange.

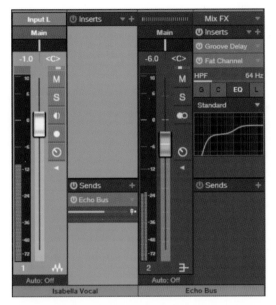

Figure 9.15 The Input channel on the left is sending some of its signal to the Echo Bus on the right. An EQ with a high-frequency boost and low-frequency cut follows the delay to shape its response.

Creating Wider-than-Life Sounds with Delay

Many signal sources are mono (voice, vintage synths, electric guitar, etc.), but can benefit from stereo imaging. Some plug-ins can make a mono track sound more like stereo through psycho-acoustic processing, but an older option is to copy a track, move it slightly behind the original track to create a short time difference between the two (e.g., around 23 ms), and then pan the two tracks oppositely. In some cases, moving the original track slightly ahead of the beat so that the two timings average out can make them sound like they're more on the beat.

How much delay to add depends on the instrument's frequency range. If the delay is too short, the two signals may cancel somewhat and create a thin sound. Lowering the copied signal's level can reduce these negative effects, but then the stereo image will be less dramatic.

 Check the combined sound of both tracks in mono. If it sounds thin or resonant, increase the delay time a little until both the stereo and mono versions are satisfactory.

If the delay is too long, you'll hear an echo effect. This can create an even wider stereo image, but there are rhythmic implications—do you *want* an audible delay? And if the delay is long enough, the sound will be more like two mono signals than a wide stereo signal.

Using Delay to Create Long, Trailing Echoes

With this effect, the echo trails off over time to provide a spacey, evocative delay. This is popular in dance music, with the delay time synched to tempo.

When used more as an effect than for thickening, the echo will likely be mixed higher, have a longer delay time, and include a significant amount of feedback to extend the trail of echoes. This can interfere with the sound that's being delayed. To restrict the echo so it occurs only when you want it (e.g., when a vocalist isn't singing), here are four options:

◆ **Send effect bus automation.** Automate the send to the echo during sections where you want echo. Vary the echo level or send bus output fader to mix the desired amount of echo in and out.

◆ **Clip effect.** Cut (split) a clip to create another clip to which you want to add echo, and insert an echo effect in the new clip. Note that the effect may stop when the clip ends. This works to your advantage if another clip follows and you want the echo to stop, but for the echo to continue, you may need to extend the clip with silence.

◆ **Split the section to be echoed to another track.** This approach's advantage is you may not have to use automation, but just set up the echo as a track plug-in. Echo will affect only the sections that are moved to that track. However, as with applying clip effects, you may need to extend the section you moved to allow the echo to continue beyond the original section length.

◆ **Plug-in automation.** Manipulate the desired controls (mainly feedback and mix), and record your automation moves. These will create automation envelopes you can edit further if needed.

Stereo Image Enhancers

These plug-ins widen or narrow stereo signals. You can turn stereo signals into super-stereo signals with an extremely wide image, or narrow them down into mono.

Most image enhancers use mid-side processing, as discussed in Chapter 7 on Equalization, to create a wider stereo image. To recap, mid-side processing separates the audio into two components, the *mid* (what's common to both channels) and the *side*, which is the difference between the two channels—basically, what's not in the center of the stereo image. However, you really don't have to think about all this, because usually there's a single control that either increases the difference signal for a wider image, or decreases it to make the image more mono. Multiband image processors include this type of control for each band (Fig. 9.16). Mid-side-based processing tends to collapse well into mono.

Figure 9.16 IK Multimedia's Quad Image multiband image enhancer plug-in splits the audio into bands (up to four). For each band, you can set the frequency split points, control the stereo width, and adjust level. The setting shown widens the stereo spread for the higher frequencies, while anchoring the bass in the center by making it more mono.

There are several applications for image enhancement. You can:

♦ Widen the overall track when mastering, to make more room in the center for the lead vocal (which is usually centered). However, making the sides more prominent may make the center seem less so.

♦ Produce a wider overall stereo image, which can help differentiate among instruments.

♦ Move the low frequencies to center in anticipation of a vinyl release, which requires that the bass be centered.

♦ Spread pads, choirs, and background vocals across the stereo mix so you can lower the overall level, yet still have their sounds be present.

Modulation Effects (Chorus, Flanger, etc.)

Modulation effects are associated more with individual instruments and pedalboards, but there are also plug-in versions for mixing. Some plug-ins provide dedicated effects for functions like chorus or flanging (Fig. 9.17). Others include a general-purpose time-delay effect that's flexible enough to provide these effects as well as others, like delay and tape echo.

Figure 9.17 This plug-in models a "vintage digital" effect—Eventide's Instant Flanger from 1976. The big knob toward the center varies the initial delay.

Chorus multiplies the sound of one instrument so it sounds like an ensemble, while flanging imparts a whooshing, jet-airplane sound that was popular in the 60s. Both these effects store the input audio in digital memory, then read the audio out a variable amount of time later (typically 15 ms or less). Modulation, created by a low-frequency oscillator that varies the delay time over a particular range, animates the sound as the delay time sweeps back and forth between a maximum and minimum value.

Chorus and Flanger Parameters

Both chorus and flanger effects have similar parameters. Here are the most common ones.

Initial Delay

This sets the base amount of delay time, generally between 0 and 15 ms. With flanging and chorusing, modulation occurs around this initial time delay. Flanging typically uses shorter initial delay times (0 to 7 ms). Chorusing uses longer initial delays (5 to 15 ms).

Balance, Mix, or Blend

Both effects depend on mixing dry and processed audio. This parameter adjusts the balance. Flanging typically uses an equal blend of dry and delayed signals, while chorusing uses more dry than delayed audio.

Feedback, Recirculation, or Regeneration

Feeding some of the output back to the input creates feedback, which gives a more defined, sharper sound—somewhat like increasing a filter's resonance control. Another option is in-phase or out-of-phase feedback; each produces a different timbre. In-phase flanging sounds sharper. Out-of-phase flanging sounds more hollow.

Sweep Range, Modulation Amount, or Depth

With flanging and chorusing, modulation causes the processed sound's pitch to go slightly flat, return to the original pitch, go slightly sharp, then return to the original pitch and start the cycle all over again. This parameter determines how much the modulation section (also called LFO, or sweep) varies the initial delay time. Sometimes the modulation sweep can sync to tempo so that the effect happens in time with the rhythm. Another option is tap tempo, where hitting a switch or button in time with the tempo sets the modulation rate.

A wide sweep range is important for dramatic flanging; chorus and echo don't need much sweep range to be effective. Note that initial delay time and modulation interact. With longer delays, too much modulation causes detuning effects.

Modulation Waveform or Shape

The modulation source usually comes from low-frequency, periodic waveforms such as triangle or square waves. However, some plug-ins include randomized waveforms, step-sequenced waveforms that sync to the song's tempo (these create sequential variations—for example, a change every 16th note), and/or envelope followers (where the modulation amount follows the incoming signal's dynamics).

Some stereo implementations of these effects may also allow reversing the modulation waveform phase in the left and right channels. For example, in one channel the flanging effect might go higher in frequency, while the other channel's frequency goes lower.

Modulation Rate

This sets the modulation frequency if it's not synched to tempo. Typical rates are 0.1 Hz (1 cycle every 10 seconds) to 15 Hz.

Voices

Found mostly in advanced chorus effects, this creates more than one chorusing path to create an effect with a more complex sound.

Modulation Effects Tips

◆ For vibrato (frequency modulation) effects, start with a short initial delay (5 ms or so), set mix for delayed sound only, and modulate the delay with a triangle or sine wave at a 3 to 14 Hz rate.

◆ To create a comb filter (a filter type that creates multiple frequency notches in the audio), choose an initial delay of 1 to 10 ms, minimum feedback, no modulation, and an equal blend of processed and straight sound.

◆ For mono to pseudo-stereo conversion, set a stereo chorus depth parameter to maximum and rate to minimum (or off). This creates a stereo spread without the spatial motion that would result from having a higher modulation rate. However, because phase cancellations may occur, make sure the sound doesn't thin out when switched to mono. If so, reduce the amount of processed sound, or increase the delay somewhat.

Where to Insert Modulation Effects

The optimum placement depends on the effect's settings, so experiment and choose what sounds best. Here are general tips:

◆ Placing these effects before distortion dilutes the effect—but you might like the way the sound cuts through the distortion.

◆ Flangers can generate massive frequency response peaks and deep valleys. You may want to follow the flanger with a limiter to restrict the dynamic range. Caution: With too much limiting, the flanging sound will be less intense.

◆ EQ placement requires experimentation. Inserting it before a flanger lets you optimize the timbre to work well with the flanging effect.

Generally, flangers, phasers, delays, reverb, and other time-based effects go toward the end of a chain of effects, prior to any loudness maximization (however when using maximization with individual tracks as described previously, you might want reverb after the maximizer).

Auto-Pan and Tremolo

Auto-pan effects sweep audio back and forth between the left and right channels. Sync to tempo is important because an out-of-sync rhythm will fight with the song's tempo. Auto-panners include many parameters of other modulation effects, like LFO speed, sync, and modulation waveforms.

Auto-panning is similar to tremolo. Auto-panning changes the levels in opposite channels so that as one channel's level increases, the other channel's level decreases; tremolo creates a periodic level change in both channels simultaneously. You'll often find auto-panning and tremolo functions combined in the same plug-in.

Tremolo is a common effect in vintage guitar amps, and was traditionally difficult to sync to the music. For a vintage sound, you may not want to sync the tremolo to tempo.

De-Esser

A de-esser is a compressor that affects only high frequencies. It's used mostly for vocals.

Although a brighter vocal can improve articulation, it can also over-emphasize "s" and "shhh" sounds. Using a de-esser to tame these occurances prior to adding other processes can keep the "s" sounds from being too shrill or prominent.

A multiband compressor or dynamic equalization can perform de-essing, but a dedicated de-esser will usually take less time to adjust.

To make editing easier, most de-essers can isolate the frequency range where de-essing will occur, so you can hear what will be de-essed. The switch to enable this is usually named something like *listen*, *audition*, or *sidechain*. Other controls will set the frequency range over which the de-essing occurs, and the amount of cut over the range.

With the listen function enabled, sweep the frequency control until you hear the sound you want to minimize. Then adjust the depth control for the desired amount of "s" reduction (Fig. 9.18).

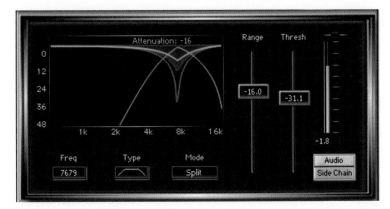

Figure 9.18 The Waves Renaissance DeEsser, set to compress frequencies around 8 kHz

After turning off the listen function, check the vocal in context with the other tracks. You may be surprised how even a little bit of de-essing can sound too drastic, so reduce the de-essing depth if needed.

With amp sims, inserting a de-esser between your guitar and an amp sim can reduce high frequencies as you play more forcefully. This acts like an intelligent version of pulling back on the tone control to create a smoother, creamier distortion sound.

Multieffects Plug-Ins

Some plug-ins contain multiple effects, like iZotope's Nectar (Fig. 9.19). It incorporates the most useful vocal processing plug-ins: De-esser, breath control, noise gate, pitch correction, reverb, slapback echo, etc.

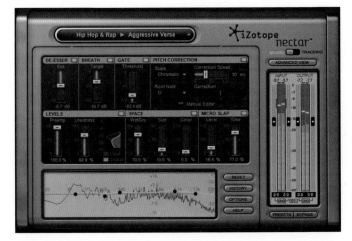

Figure 9.19 iZotope's Nectar is like a "greatest hits" of vocal processors in a single plug-in.

The artist plug-in is another variation on this concept. Popularized by Waves, producers like Butch Vig, Eddie Kramer, Manny Marroquin, Tony Maserati, and others work with a manufacturer to create plug-ins with the signal processing chains they use for vocals, drums, bass, and other audio sources (Fig. 9.20).

Figure 9.20 The Butch Vig Vocals plug-in includes EQ, filters, compression, de-essing, saturation, and other processors Butch uses to obtain his vocal sounds.

The controls are often macros that edit several parameters at once so that it's easy to obtain the sounds the producers intended. You can then modify them, although not as much as if they were a collection of individual plug-ins.

Pitch Correction

Pitch correction has somewhat of a bad reputation. When used properly, listeners don't know it's there—but when used improperly, it can make vocals sound unnatural and in some cases, annoying. The key to transparent pitch correction is to correct only notes that sound wrong. If the correction has to be so severe that a note sounds unnatural, you are better served by re-recording that part of the vocal.

 Some singers are more daring with their vocals, knowing that they can use pitch correction to fix the occasional wrong note when mixing. Purists often say pitch correction takes the soul out of a vocal, but it can also have the opposite effect, by freeing an artist from concentrating on the pitch more than the performance—which can also take the soul out of a vocal.

The big names in pitch correction are Antares Auto-Tune and Celemony Melodyne; however pitch correction plug-ins from companies like iZotope and Waves are also available, and several recording programs (e.g., Cubase, Logic, Digital Performer) include their own type of pitch correction. Most of these programs also allow you to edit timing so you can alter the phrasing.

How Pitch Correction Works

Automatic pitch correction software analyzes pitches in audio, compares detected pitches to the correct scale frequencies, and then raises or lowers the pitches to quantize them to the correct frequencies (Fig. 9.21). You can also move notes manually, which is important—sometimes you don't want a note to hit exactly on pitch, but perhaps be a bit flat to add tension.

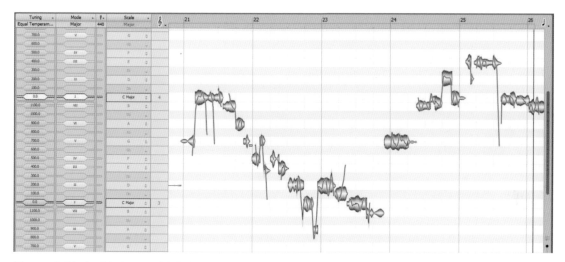

Figure 9.21 In this image, Melodyne has analyzed a vocal performance and displays "blobs" where notes have been detected. The notes on the left half have been corrected so they're quantized to the pitch scale on the left; the notes on the right (after measure 24) have not been corrected.

Most pitch correction is monophonic and works only on single-note lines like vocal, wind instruments, bass, etc. However, higher-end Melodyne versions can do polyphonic pitch correction, which is pretty amazing. If one note in a guitar chord is out of tune, Melodyne can fix that one note.

The analysis data can also create MIDI notes. For example, you could play a bass part on guitar, convert that to MIDI data using pitch correction software, transpose the part down an octave, and then use it to trigger a synth bass. Audio-to-MIDI conversion (especially polyphonic) isn't perfect, but some time spent cleaning up the MIDI data will give the desired results.

Applying Pitch Correction

There's not much to pitch correction. Either you turn off pitch quantization and click/drag notes manually, or you select notes and snap them to the scale. Like rhythmic quantization, varying quantization strength moves the pitch closer to being corrected without snapping exactly to the "perfect" pitch.

Other Pitch Correction Applications

Pitch correction can do more than fix out-of-tune vocals. Here are some possibilities.

Automatic Double-Tracking (ADT) for Vocals

Before applying pitch correction to a vocal, copy it. If you plan to do pitch correction, apply correction only to the original vocal. Then open the copied vocal in your pitch correction software, and add a *slight* amount of pitch and timing correction (Fig. 9.22).

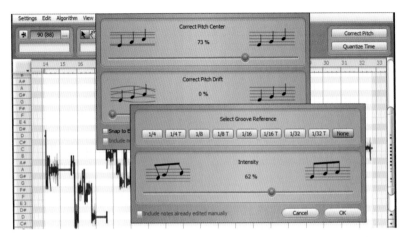

Figure 9.22 The copied clip has a little bit of pitch and time correction compared to the original clip. This creates the slight differences needed for an automatic double-tracking effect.

The slight pitch and timing differences can make the copied vocal sound like a double-tracked vocal compared to the original one. You can take this further with Melodyne's Editor version by making subtle formant changes, and/or adding random pitch and timing deviations.

Add a Harmony

Although this probably should have been handled before the mixing stage, pitch correction software can provide harmonies. A real vocal is best, but synthesized harmonies can work surprisingly well.

Copy the original vocal track from which you want to create the harmony. Adjust the copy's pitches to create the desired harmony (Fig. 9.23).

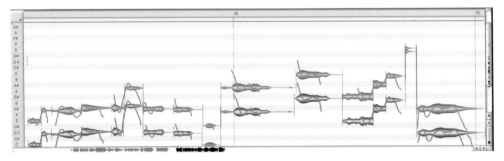

Figure 9.23 The orange blobs represent the original vocal. The blue ones were copied from the harmony track, colored blue for contrast, and pasted on a screenshot of the original vocal to make it easier to see the difference.

The sound quality will not equal the original vocal, but if you mix the harmony in the background, it will probably be good enough. And if the harmony was missing from the mix because it was out of the singer's range, synthesizing a harmony can be the answer.

Create Heavy Drum Sounds

To add meat to wimpy drum sounds, copy the drum track, and then drop the pitch several semitones. Mix this about 6 dB lower than the main track, and behold—instant drum corpulence. You can also "tighten" drum sounds, particularly kick and toms, by raising the copied pitch a couple semitones.

Full, Tight Kick Drums

Make two copies of a kick track. Tune one up three semitones, and tune the other down two semitones for a full, tight kick. Vary pitch more if you dare, but this can loosen the timing.

Octave Divider Bass

Pitch correction software can create decent octave-below effects. Copy your bass track, select all the duplicate audio, and drag it down one octave. For best results, use EQ on the copied track to take off most of the highs and boost the bass. This technique is particularly helpful when you need to play the bass in a higher range than you'd like in order to accommodate a particular key, and want some more low-end authority. You don't need to mix in too much of the octave signal to add some fatness.

Pitch Uncorrection

The human ear is not always a fan of perfection. I recorded two backup vocals that just didn't seem quite right, but their pitches—and those of the track underneath it—were accurate. But that's what wasn't right. Selectively flattening the pitch of a few notes in the background vocals made the sound far more interesting.

Where to Insert Pitch Correction

Pitch correction wants the driest, plainest sound possible. Place the pitch correction first in any signal chain. The only exception is a de-esser—reducing high frequency sounds can improve the pitch correction analysis.

Pitch Transposer

These have generally been replaced by pitch correction software. Pitch transposer plug-ins synthesize a harmony line from an input signal. Simple pitch transposers are limited to parallel harmonies, while more sophisticated versions produce "intelligent" harmonies based on the rules of harmony for a specified scale (Fig. 9.24).

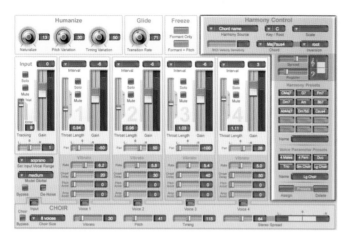

Figure 9.24   Antares' Harmony Engine EVO is a vocal processor that generates up to four harmony lines. Although it can generate harmonies automatically, if it generates wrong notes, you can use MIDI to specify the harmonies.

If your transposer doesn't offer "intelligent" harmonization, you may still be able to change the transposition amount using MIDI notes or continuous controllers.

A pitch transposer essentially cuts a signal into little pieces, then glues the pieces back together in (mostly) real time so that they take up less time (shifting pitch up) or more time (shifting pitch down). Typical parameters include the transposition interval, mix to set the balance of dry and transposed signals, and for intelligent transposers, the key and mode. Some also include feedback to feed some of the output back to the input. This creates stepped harmonies and other special effects.

Like anything else that changes pitch, the more drastic the transposition, the greater the risk of generating artifacts like a fluctuating tremolo effect, glitches, or a rough vocal character.

Pitch transposers can produce excellent flanging/chorusing effects. Set the pitch control for a very slight amount of transposition (1 to 20 cents or so), and mix the transposed signal with the dry version.

Exciter

The original exciters were introduced during tape's heyday. Tape has a problem with self-erasure—the more you run tape, the more the high frequencies deteriorate. Exciters filtered out all but the very highest frequencies, then distorted them to create high-frequency harmonics. Mixing this in parallel with a track or a final mix added a desirable kind of sparkle and presence (Fig. 9.25).

Figure 9.25 The Aphex Vintage Aural Exciter from Waves models the original hardware exciter introduced in the mid-70s. The demand for the original units was so high, they were available only as expensive rentals.

The concept is still useful with sounds that lack high-frequency content, but where EQ is too heavy-handed. Exciters can also lift an individual track out of the mix with no significant level increase. Be sparing with an exciter effect. It adds a boost in the range where instruments normally don't have a lot of energy, so exciter-based processing can stand out quite a bit.

Restoration Plug-Ins

Hopefully, you'll never need to use restoration plug-ins, but sometimes tracks will have crackles, pops, or hiss. Restoration plug-ins tend toward heavy CPU consumption, and you may not be able to monitor them in real time. Instead, render the tracks and then undo the change if you don't like the results; or render offline with a program that can work stand-alone, such as iZotope RX.

An unconventional use for de-crackling plug-ins that reduce vinyl surface noise is to smooth out the sound of amp sims.

Multiband Processing

This isn't a specific effect, but a way of processing that works with various effects. We already met multiband processing with the multiband compressor discussed in Chapter 8. Multiband processing splits a signal into multiple frequency bands—e.g., lows, lower mids, upper mids, and highs—and then processes each band individually. With hardware, this is complex, expensive, and difficult to implement. But in today's software-based world, multiband processing is easy to do, and it opens up new ways to shape sound during the mix.

The easiest multiband processing uses a processor designed for this purpose. For example, Steinberg's Quadrafuzz 2 (Fig. 9.26) is a multiband distortion plug-in.

Figure 9.26 Steinberg's Quadrafuzz 2 virtualizes the four-band Quadrafuzz hardware distortion unit I designed back in the 80s.

Multiband processing is effective with distortion. Split a guitar into different bands and then distort each one individually for a more defined, articulated tone. When you hit a low open string and then play a solo high on the neck, the two won't interfere with each other but sound distinct.

However, it's possible to create a multiband processing setup for any effect. For example, with delay you might not want to delay *all* frequencies—delaying low frequencies might add "mud" that doesn't happen when you delay only the upper mids and treble. Also, long delays on the higher frequency bands and shorter, slapback-type delays on low-frequency bands may create a delay effect that fits better in a track. And splitting an instrument into four bands, then chorusing each one separately, can give gorgeous, lush chorusing effects.

There are three main steps in creating a multiband effects setup.

Step 1: Create Parallel Signal Chains (Splits)

You'll need parallel signal paths for as many bands as you plan to use. Let's assume four-band multiband processing because that's often all you need.

Some devices already have parallel paths, like the Line 6 Helix (Fig. 9.27). Splitting the input to the four parallel path in Helix provides four bands of parallel processing. This works with both the Helix floor processor and the Helix Native plug-in version.

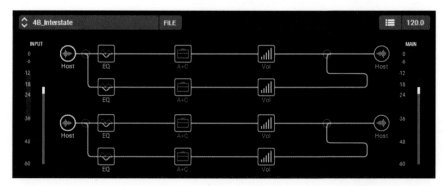

Figure 9.27 This preset creates multiband distortion using amp sims.

Some host programs can create parallel signal paths. Studio One provides a split module; however, you can also split one of the split paths into more splits. For example, one split module can feed two more split modules for four parallel paths (Fig. 9.28).

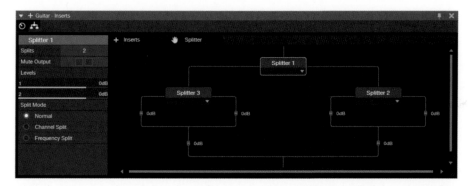

Figure 9.28 Use the Normal mode in Studio One's Splitter to send the same signal to both splits. This example shows four parallel paths.

Some plug-ins, like Native Instruments' Guitar Rig, can do splits. For the four-band phasing preset shown in Figure 9.29, a Guitar Rig splitter (the split with green lettering) is sending Split A into another split (outlined in blue). This splits into two bands, each with an equalizer to restrict the frequency range, and a phaser to provide the effect. Split B goes into another split (outlined in yellow). This also splits into two more bands, each with an equalizer and phaser. The Split Mix at the bottom combines the four splits back into a stereo signal.

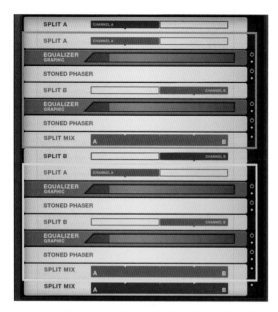

Figure 9.29 Guitar Rig's split function allows for splits within splits.

A less elegant option is to use sends and busses to create parallel paths, with each bus serving as one path. This works well if the host program has accurate plug-in delay compensation so the tracks remain in sync. However, you still need to create frequency bands for each send (see next section).

The least elegant way to create multiband processing is to copy a track as many times as you want bands, create the frequency bands, and then insert the appropriate effects into each track. As with using send FX, the program will need good plug-in delay compensation.

Step 2: Create Frequency Bands

Now we need to create our bands. Although some splits in software programs can split by frequency, these are usually just *crossovers* that separate a signal into two bands—everything below and above a certain frequency. When needing more than two bands, I use multiband compression set to not compress.

Here's how this process works:

1. However you obtained the splits, insert a multiband compressor in one of the splits, and listen to only this split (i.e., solo it if possible). Set the compression ratio for all bands to 1:1. This defeats compression so the plug-in can become a multiband crossover.

2. Solo each band in this multiband compressor, and adjust each band's high and low boundaries to cover the desired frequency ranges.

3. Save these multiband compressor settings as a temporary preset. Insert an instance of the multiband compressor into each split, and call up the temporary preset for each instance.

4. Solo the lowest band on one split, the lower mids on another split, the upper mids on another split, and the highs on another split. This will restrict each split to a particular frequency band (Fig. 9.30).

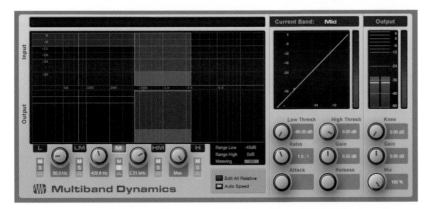

Figure 9.30 This screenshot shows Studio One's Multiband Dynamics set up as one band of a four-band crossover, with the midrange band soloed and the other bands muted.

If multiband compressors aren't available, you can use graphic equalizer processors for splits. For example, with the Line 6 Helix Native plug-in, for the lows I turn up the bottom three bands and set the other bands to minimum. For the low mids, I turn up the 250 Hz and 500 Hz bands while the rest are turned down, and so on (Fig. 9.31). Using a graphic EQ to split guitar can sometimes be more flexible than using multiband compression because you can "bleed" some audio from one band into another band if it improves the sound.

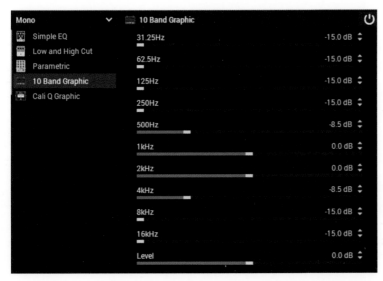

Figure 9.31 The Helix's graphic EQ is boosting the midrange bands while cutting the other bands.

Step 3: Start Processing

Once you've created your multiband setup by making splits and isolating frequency bands, the fun begins.

 Because it takes some effort to set up an environment for multiband processing, if your program can save track presets or track templates, you should save your multiband layout so you can call it up when needed.

For each split, you may want to include the same processor but with different settings. Or you might want processors in some splits but not others (e.g., octave divider on only the low frequencies and octave multiplier on only the high frequencies). Or you might use completely different processors in each split.

If you haven't played with multiband processing, give it a try. You might be surprised at where it takes you... and your mix.

Key Takeaways

♦ Console emulation is a subtle effect, but don't knock it until you've tried it.

♦ Tape emulation can indeed emulate the sound of tape. However, it's simply a different type of processing, not necessarily something magical.

♦ Don't overlook distortion as a mixing tool. It can help make bass and kick drum more prominent in a mix.

♦ Delay effects synchronized to tempo are a staple of many dance mixes. This is particularly effective when there's an option to control the EQ in the feedback loop so successive repeats are less bright.

♦ Synchronizing delay times to tempo is a common way of setting delay times in modern productions.

♦ Stereo image enhancers are best when used sparingly on individual tracks. Note that they expand outward by leaving more of a "hole" in the center, which can be useful to avoid interference with other sounds that are panned to the center (voice, snare, etc.).

♦ Chorusing tends to diffuse the sound, which can place instruments more in the background. This might be what you want, but could also be problematic—use caution.

♦ De-essers are helpful with vocals to add clarity and articulation because they can remove objectionable "s" sounds prior to increasing the overall high frequency response.

♦ Pitch correction gets a bad rap, but mostly because it's overused. If you use it tastefully, the result can be better vocals that still sound natural.

♦ If a track lacks "sparkle," try an exciter plug-in to give it a treble increase that's less harsh than EQ.

♦ Restoration plug-ins can remove pops, hiss, and clicks that could mar otherwise excellent tracks.

♦ Multiband processing allows for more nuanced effects, and works particularly well with distortion.

Chapter 10

Creating a Stereo Soundstage

Now we have our tracks squared away: they sound great, they all carve out their part of the frequency spectrum, their levels are well balanced, and some of them even have some cool effects. But there is more to do yet.

We hear live music in an acoustic space. Our ears receive cues that locate instruments closer to us or farther away, and to the right, left, or center. We also receive cues from the back and front. One of mixing's goals is to create a convincing *soundstage* (acoustical environment) in which we hear the recorded music. Your goal might be traditional—to re-create the feel of a live performance—or to ignore reality completely, and create a space that could exist only in a virtual world.

The main ways to do this involve panning (the placement of sounds in the stereo field) and using reverberation and delay, which emulate an acoustical space. Although the spatial options of mixing in stereo are limited to left, right, or somewhere in between, placing sounds in a soundfield is an important part of mixing—so let's start with panning.

Panning Basics

Your mixer's channel strip will typically have a *panpot* (short for panoramic potentiometer) that places instruments within the stereo field (Fig. 10.1). Different applications approach pan controls in different ways.

Figure 10.1 *Four different panpot approaches. Left to right: Traditional panpots at top of channel strip (Samplitude), sliders (Studio One), separate panpots for left and right channels (Pro Tools), and panpot with width control for stereo tracks along with conventional panpot for mono tracks (Reason).*

Stereo placement alters how we perceive a sound. Consider a doubled vocal line, where a singer sings a part and then doubles it as closely as possible. Panning the parts to center gives a somewhat smoother sound, which is good for weaker vocalists. Spreading the parts more left and right to create a stereo image gives a more defined sound. This can help accent a good singer.

Also note that you can automate panning—an instrument needn't have a static location throughout a song. For example, you might start with a percussion instrument panned to center, but when a second percussion instrument enters the mix toward the right, you could alter the first percussion part so it tilts toward the left. With parts in a mix's background, these changes won't be distracting—they'll be sensed more than heard.

How Panning Differs for Stereo and Mono Tracks

With most programs, the pan control works differently for stereo and mono audio tracks, as well as for MIDI data:

♦ Pan places a mono track at a specific point within the stereo field—anywhere from full left to full right.

♦ With stereo tracks, the panpot becomes a balance control. Moving the panpot off center to the right turns down the left channel until, when all the way to the right, you hear the right channel only. Moving the panpot toward the left makes the right channel progressively softer and the left channel progressively louder.

Pro Tools treats stereo signals as two mono signals, each with its own panpot, so the signal can spread over any part of the stereo field. For example, with two stereo rhythm guitar parts, one part could span the range from left to center, while the other spans the range from center to right. This still gives a stereo image but keeps the guitars spatially separate. However, this approach requires more time to set up panning.

Some other programs have a plug-in that can pan the right and left channels independently (Fig. 10.2), or you may need to split a stereo track into two mono tracks to change the pan and level independently for each channel.

Figure 10.2 Studio One's Dual Pan plug-in provides independent pan control over the left and right channels. It has five different panning curves that determine how the amplitude changes as you pan from left to right. –3 dB Constant Power Sin/Cos keeps the perceived volume constant while panning.

Panning and MIDI

The MIDI specification assigns continuous controller #10 to panning. With MIDI tracks, a mixer's pan control sends these messages to tell a MIDI instrument where to place the audio. Any plug-in that recognizes this controller will react to it. When controlling outboard gear, you can create a pan envelope in a MIDI track, and then send this MIDI data to a MIDI output port that patches into the hardware gear.

Panning Tips

There's more to panning than just stereo placement. These tips can optimize a project's panning:

♦ **Panning bass frequencies.** Because bass frequencies are less directional than highs, most engineers place the kick drum and bass toward the center (unless the bass is a synth type and recorded in stereo).

♦ **Panning high frequencies.** Highs are very directional, so placing higher frequency instruments (shaker, tambourine) further to the left or right helps give the illusion of a wider stereo field.

♦ **Extreme panning doesn't always work.** I generally don't pan to the *extreme* left or right, but always pan at least a little bit toward center. If the sound is full right or left, it will come from only a single point source and sound less realistic.

♦ **Consider timbral balance when panning.** If you've panned a hi-hat (which has lots of high frequencies) to the right, pan other high-frequency sounds (e.g., tambourine or shaker) somewhat to the left. The same concept applies to any instruments with overlapping frequency ranges.

♦ **MIDI panning.** Panning an instrument sound back and forth with an LFO may sound gimmicky because you hear an audible sweep. Modulating panning with velocity can sound much more natural. By using this technique, when you first hit a note its stereo position will be determined by the velocity, and the sustain will retain that location in the stereo field until replayed.

♦ **Locate sounds in space.** When you play the piano, there's a sense of lower notes emanating from the left, and higher notes from the right. You'll probably want a similar spread when mixing, at least for solo piano.

♦ **Audience perspective or performer perspective.** As you set up stereo placement for instruments, think about your listener's position. For a drummer, the high-hat is on the left, and the toms on the right, but for the audience, it's the reverse. I generally go for the performer's perspective from force of habit (a habit I'm trying to break!).

♦ **Synthesizer splits.** Synthesizers with *split* functionality (i.e., the ability to split keyboard sections to play different sounds) can enhance spatial placement. One option if you're handling the bass line with your left hand is to send the lowest split with the bass to the center, a middle split to left of center, and the top split to right of center. This is not necessarily the most realistic option for imitating the real world, but hey—it's a synth. If there's already a bass part, try spreading the synthesizer sound from left to right, going from lower keys to higher keys. This keeps your low frequencies spatially separated from the bass.

♦ **Synthesizer pan modulation.** The easiest way to spread a keyboard is if a key range can tie panning to note number. This creates a wide spread when the synthesizer's output feeds a stereo mixer channel. However, unless the keyboard is the major focus of the music, you'll probably want to narrow the range somewhat. For example, if guitar is another major melodic instrument, try spreading the guitar from left of center to center and the keyboard from center to right of center.

♦ **Panning and Delay.** Placing a delayed sound in the same spatial location as the main sound may cause the echoes to obscure the main notes. To avoid this, if your instrument is weighted to one side of the stereo spread, weight the delayed sound (set to delayed only/no dry signal) to the other side of the spread. If you're using stereo delay on a lead instrument that's panned to center, try panning one channel of echo toward the left, and the other toward the right.

Also, polyrhythmic echoes can give lively "ping-pong" effects. Of course, this may sound gimmicky (not always a bad thing!) but if the echoes are mixed relatively low and there's some stereo reverb, the sense of spaciousness can be huge.

♦ **Panning with two mics on a single instrument.** For a bigger sound when using two mics on a single instrument, pan the right mic track full right, the left mic track full left, then duplicate the right and left mic tracks. Pan the duplicated tracks to center, and then bring the duplicated tracks down about 5 to 6 dB (or to taste). This fills in the center hole that normally occurs by panning the two main signals to the extreme left and right. Also experiment with adding reverb in different ways—only the main channels, only the middle channels, weighted toward the left or weighted toward the right, etc.

Binaural Panning

Although stereo can provide only left, center, and right positioning, some processes can emulate the effect of listening in an acoustical space where you sense sounds as being from above, below, and behind.

For example, when listening through headphones, your left ear will hear the left channel, and your right ear will hear the right channel. However, with loudspeakers your left ear will hear the left channel, but so will your right ear—at a reduced volume, with filtering due to the sound going past your head, and slightly later because it's farther away from the left speaker than the left ear. Various products emulate this phenomenon to give the effect of listening over loudspeakers when wearing headphones. This is handy if you're mixing on the road with a laptop, and want to hear what the mix might sound like over speakers.

Binaural panning is rather loosely defined; it's a technique that's most effective when listening on headphones. Binaural panners range from the simple to the complex. Studio One's implementation is fairly simple; it uses mid-side processing to separate the center and left/right channels, and can create a wider-than-stereo effect with stereo tracks.

The binaural panner in Apple's Logic Pro X is more complex, unique to that program, and provides precise sound field positioning (Fig. 10.3).

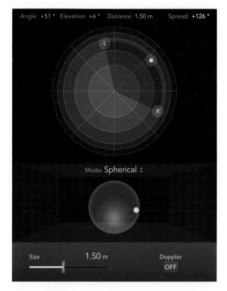

Figure 10.3 Logic Pro X's binaural panner adds a psycho-acoustic effect that conventional panning can't do. This mode creates a spherical space in which you can place a sound.

The Audio Architect: Building Your Acoustical Space

You can build an acoustical space in which your song lives by adding reverberation and delay to give depth to the normally flat soundstage. It's common for an overall reverb to create a particular type of space (club, concert hall, auditorium, etc.). You may also want a second reverb to add effects, such as a particular "splash" on a snare drum hit, gated reverb on toms, or super-diaphanous reverb on vocals.

Vocals often have a separate reverb because they're mixed front and center, and it can be desirable to optimize a reverb sound specifically for vocals.

In the early days of recording, most engineers added enough reverb to be noticeable and simulate the effect of playing in an acoustical environment. However, modern reverb devices have become so sophisticated, they can create effects that become as much a part of a tune as any instrumental line.

If a part is questionable, reverb can't salvage it. A bad part with lots of reverb is still a bad part—to paraphrase Nike, just re-do it.

About Reverb

If a room's acoustics are baked into a recording, there's little you can do to remove those characteristics. Although studios often strive to provide a neutral, dry-sounding environment, a *totally* dry sound goes against our expectation of hearing music in an acoustic space. In addition, some studios have rooms that are purposely not neutral because they have a particularly desirable sound.

The Different Reverb Types

Originally, reverb was provided by a physical space, like a concrete chamber built for this purpose. Perhaps the most famous example is the reverb setup designed by Les Paul for the Capitol Records studios in Los Angeles. He specified eight concrete echo chambers, each with specific sonic characteristics, dug 30 feet into the ground—no other reverb sounds like this. Another famous example of reverb is the Olympian drum sound on Led Zeppelin's "When the Levee Breaks," which was the result of John Bonham's kit having room mics set up in a three-story stairwell. Sonic Vista Studios in Ibiza, Spain has an incredible reverb sound thanks to a centuries-old well used as a reverb chamber.

Although you can't fit a concert hall in your project studio, it's possible to model acoustic spaces with surprising realism—as well as model the sound of classic gear, and even create virtual spaces that can't exist in real life.

There are two main electronic reverb technologies.

Synthesized Reverb

Synthesized reverb (also called *algorithmic* reverb) ruled the digital reverb world for several decades. This technology recreates the reverb effect with three processes:

♦ *Pre-delay* emulates the time it takes for a signal to travel from the source to the first reflective surfaces.

♦ *Early reflections* are the initial sounds that happen when sound waves first bounce off room surfaces.

♦ *Decay* is the wash of sound caused by emulating the myriad reflections that occur in a real room, with their various amplitude and frequency response variations (see Fig. 10.4).

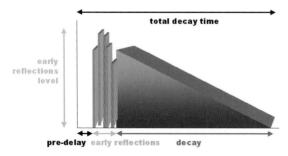

Figure 10.4 Synthesized reverb deconstructs reverb into these parameters.

Many, if not most, digital reverbs are not true stereo devices. They mix stereo inputs into mono, and synthesize a stereo space. This is why you can obtain stereo reverb effects with a mono signal like voice.

Convolution Reverb

Convolution reverb is like taking an audio snapshot of an acoustic space's characteristics, and then superimposing those characteristics onto your audio. As an analogy, think of the impulse as a "mold" of a particular space that you pour the sound into. If the space is a concert hall, then the sound takes on the characteristics of the concert hall. This produces a highly realistic sound, much like how a keyboard sampler can produce more realistic sounds than a keyboard synthesizer.

The tradeoff for this realism is the usual sampler vs. synthesizer issue: difficulty in editing the sounds. However, many modern convolution reverbs are quite editable, and as easy to use and understand as standard reverbs. Changing parameters may feel sluggish due to all the calculations being performed, but this isn't a deal-breaker. Thanks to today's faster processors, convolution reverbs are common. Choosing convolution or synthesized reverb is a matter of taste (Fig. 10.5), and many programs include both.

Figure 10.5 The reverb on the left is Studio One's Open Air reverb, while the reverb on the right is their algorithmic Room Reverb.

To generalize, synthesized reverb can give a more diaphanous, airy type of sound, while convolution delivers a more realistic, you-are-there kind of vibe. It's kind of like the difference between an impressionistic painting and a photograph—both can give enjoyment, for different reasons.

One Reverb or Many?

Back in recording's stone age, a recording had one reverb, and all channel sends were bussed to it. The vocals usually sent more signal than some of the other instruments, but the result was a cohesive group sound.

Later on, studios often used a specific reverb for vocals to make the voice more distinctive. A studio's *plate reverb* (an early type of mechanical reverb) was frequently the reverb of choice because it usually had a brighter, crisper sound than a traditional room reverb. This complemented voice well, which tends not to have a lot of high-frequency response.

With the advent of inexpensive digital reverb, some people went crazy—one reverb type on the voice, gated reverb on drums, some gauzy reverb on guitars, and maybe even one or two reverbs in an aux bus. The result bears no resemblance to the real world. That's not necessarily a bad thing, but if taken to extremes, your ears—which know what acoustical spaces sound like—recognize the sound as artificial. Unless you're going for a novelty effect, this can be a problem.

If your digital reverb has a convincing plate algorithm, try that as a channel insert effect on vocals, and use a good room or hall reverb in an aux bus for your other signals. To help create a smoother blend, send some of the vocal reverb to the main reverb. This will likely require dialing back the dedicated vocal track reverb level a bit because the main reverb will add to the vocal reverb level (see Fig. 10.6).

Figure 10.6 This mixer routing in Pro Tools shows a Universal Audio EMT 140 plate reverb inserted in the vocal path, but with an additional send (the white button marked "verb") going to the main hall reverb that processes the other instruments.

Supplementing Reverb with a Real Acoustic Space

Although the sound quality of digital reverbs has increased dramatically since they were first introduced, there's nothing quite like a physical acoustic space. But you don't need a concert hall to obtain a good reverb sound. Even relatively small spaces, if they're reflective enough, can provide a useful ambiance. For example, you can send an aux bus out to a speaker in your bathroom, place a mic in the bathroom, and bring its output back into a mixer input.

 You can modify the bathroom's acoustics by adding or removing towels, and opening or closing the shower curtain.

Send some of your vocal channel's digital reverb output through an aux bus into this space, and return just enough of the acoustical reverb to provide the equivalent of "sonic caulking" to the digital reverb sound. The room will add more complex early reflections than all but the very best digital reverbs. You might be surprised at how much this can enhance the sound.

Also consider adding some feedback to the room reverb by sending some of the room reverb return back into the send output feeding the speaker. Caution: keep the monitors at extremely low levels as you experiment—you *don't* want a major feedback blast.

Reverb Parameters and Controls

A sophisticated reverb has many parameters, and it's not always obvious how to optimize these for specific recording situations. Here are some guidelines—but as always, there are no rules.

Early Reflections

Also called *initial reflections*, the associated parameters control the time between when a sound occurs and when the sound waves hit walls, ceilings, etc. These reflections tend to sound more like discrete echoes than reverb. The early reflections time is usually variable from 0 to around 100 ms. A level parameter sets a balance with the overall reverb decay. Increase the time to give the feeling of a bigger space; for example, you may want to complement a large room size with a reasonable amount of pre-delay.

- With vocals, I prefer not to use a lot of early reflections or pre-delay so that the vocal stands out.

- With drums, rhythm guitar, piano, and other primarily percussive instruments, the secondary percussive attack from the early reflections can be distracting if the reverb's level is fairly high. A short amount of pre-delay mixed behind the main reverb decay can work well. However, if you're trying for a more intimate, ensemble sound, consider avoiding pre-delay.

- Pads and sounds with long attacks, like a distant flute or brass, often benefit from pre-delay to place them further back in the soundstage.

Decay Time and Decay Time Frequencies

Decay is the sound created by the reflections as they bounce around a space. This "wash" of sound, also called the reverb tail, is what most people associate with reverb. The decay time parameter determines how long it takes for the reflections to run out of energy and become inaudible. Long reverb times may sound impressive on instruments when soloed, but they rarely work in a mix unless the arrangement is sparse.

Many reverbs offer a *crossover frequency,* which divides the reverb into high and low frequency ranges. You can specify separate decay times (abbreviated RT) for high and low frequencies. To prevent interfering with midrange instruments, consider using less decay on the lower frequencies and longer decay on the highs. With vocals this adds "air" and emphasizes some of the sibilants and mouth noises that humanize a vocal; with drums it emphasizes stick hits. It can also bring out an acoustic guitar's percussive attack. Vary the crossover setting to determine what works best for a particular signal (see Fig. 10.7).

Figure 10.7 The Breverb reverb from Overloud has separate decay times and programmable frequencies for the high and low bands.

If your reverb sounds overly metallic, try reducing the highs starting at 4 to 8 kHz. Many of the great-sounding plate reverbs didn't have much response above 5 kHz, so don't worry if your reverb doesn't provide high frequency brilliance. Reducing low frequencies (below 100 to 200 Hz) going into reverb can reduce muddiness and increase definition.

All these controls impact the overall reverb character. Increasing the low frequency decay creates a bigger, more massive sound. Lengthening high frequency decay gives a more ethereal effect. With few exceptions this is not the way high-frequency sounds work in nature, but an extended high-frequency decay can sound excellent with vocals because in addition to adding more reverb to sibilants and fricatives, it minimizes reverb on plosives and lower vocal ranges.

Diffusion

A reverb's diffusion control increases the density ("thickness") of the echoes. High diffusion places echoes closer together, while low diffusion spreads them out.

With percussive sounds, low diffusion creates lots of tightly spaced attacks, like marbles hitting steel. But with voice, which is more sustained, low diffusion can blend well—high diffusion settings may sound overly thick (see Fig. 10.8).

Figure 10.8 Low diffusion settings, as shown here in the Waves Renaissance Reverb, are often—but not always—preferable for vocals compared to high diffusion settings.

However, with less complex material, you might want more diffusion on the vocals for a richer sound. For example, plate reverbs are popular with vocals because of their high diffusion characteristics. As always... no rules.

Reverb Algorithm

With synthesized reverbs, the algorithm is a fancy name for the type of space being emulated. Typical algorithms synthesize halls, rooms, vintage synthetic reverbs, cathedrals, gymnasiums, closets—anything is possible. There are even *reverse reverb* algorithms where the decay builds up from nothing to full volume rather than decaying from full volume to nothing. *Gated reverb* algorithms cut off the reverb tail abruptly below a certain level (this effect was very popular in the 80s on drums).

With convolution reverbs, the equivalent to an algorithm is the *impulse*. Impulses capture the sound of specific rooms (like particular concert halls or recording studio rooms), but it's also possible to create impulses of older hardware reverbs.

Tech Talk: The Convolution Process

Although well suited to reverb, convolution impulses can include speaker cabinets, guitar bodies, equalizer responses—just about anything. There are lots of impulses available for download from the web (many are free) that can load into convolution reverb processors. It's even possible to create your own impulses; I've created several using white noise, which can give excellent reverb sounds if you shape the frequency response and decay characteristics. Convolution-based processors can also import just about any kind of audio file and apply convolution; experiment with loading drum loops, individual instrument notes, and sound effects—the results can be surprising and sometimes useful.

Room Size

This affects the length of the paths taken by the waves while bouncing around in the virtual room. Just like real rooms, artificial rooms can have resonances and some frequencies where the reflections cancel or add to each other. If the reverb sound has excessive *flutter* (a periodic warbling effect), vary this parameter in conjunction with decay time (described previously) for the smoothest sound.

Damping

When sounds bounce around in a hall with hard surfaces, the reverb's decay will be bright and present. With softer surfaces (e.g., wood instead of concrete, or a hall filled with people), the reverb tails will lose high frequencies as they bounce around, producing a warmer sound. If your reverb can't create a smooth-sounding high end, increase damping to place the focus more on the midrange and lower frequencies.

Create Virtual Room Mics with Delay

Along with reverb, another common technique for giving a sense of space is room mics. These mics are placed at a distance from the sound source to capture sound in the room while recording. Room mics add ambiance and enhance the stereo image; by doing only close miking or direct injection recording, we lose that sense of space. The lack of room mics is particularly noticeable when mixing a combination of instruments recorded direct in combination with miked instruments. The direct tracks sometimes won't mesh with the other sounds.

Room mics add short, discrete echoes. To simulate this effect, split the audio into multiple parallel delays, set for short times and delayed sound only. This does a credible job of emulating the waveform cancellations and additions caused by room reflections. This effect is so associated with the sound of miking an instrument in a small room that our brains think "Aha! This was recorded in a small room!"

The Setup

Although you can use as many delays as you want, four delays is often sufficient. Set the four delay times to 11, 13, 17, and 23 ms. These prime numbers won't create resonances with each other.

If your delay times can't go short enough, try using a chorus. Many chorus effects can provide short delays, as set by the Initial Delay control. Use dry sound only, with little, if any modulation (which in any case should be very slow).

With mono delays, you'll need four busses. Using stereo delays that offer individual delay times for the left and right channels allows you to reduce this to two busses. Programs that allow for parallel inserts (Fig. 10.9) let you do this with a single bus.

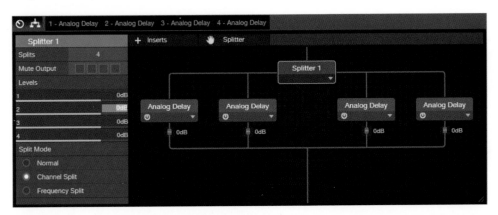

Figure 10.9 Studio One includes a splitter as an insert for routing signals. In this example one split feeds two delays in the left channel, while the other feeds two delays in the right channel.

Editing Parameters Other than Delay Times

- **Panning.** If you can pan the delays, try panning the short delays closer to center, and the longer delays more left and right. Experiment—even small changes in pan and delay settings can make a big difference in the sound.

- **Feedback.** More feedback gives more diffusion, at least up until the point where the sound takes on a resonant quality. You'll likely want more feedback with percussive instruments like drums than with sustained instruments. Too much feedback sounds unrealistic.

- **Damping.** Unless you want to sound like the room's walls have super-hard surfaces, use damping to reduce the brightness of the echoes. Some delays include filters so you can do this within the plug-in.

- **Modulation.** For delays that can produce modulation, a very subtle amount adds animation.

Additional Short Delay Tips

- To change the pseudo-room characteristics, try other delay times between 1 and 15 ms, as well as different modulation depths and rates.

If available, use modulation to vary delay times. Changing delay times with automation generally will not work as it can produce clicks and other artifacts.

- Beware of phase cancellations if you add in too much delayed signal. Although the goal is to re-create the phase cancellation/addition effects found in rooms, high levels of processed signal can cause excessive cancellation. Solo the track being processed along with the delays and then check the main output bus output in mono to confirm that the sound is still acceptable.

- Mixing in just a little bit of delay is sufficient to create a more realistic sound for the listener.

- With mostly mono source material, this technique will tend to give better stereo imaging. With stereo source material, using short delays may collapse the field and make the stereo spread less obvious. Sometimes this is a benefit as it provides an overall sonic ambiance for instruments like drums.

- These types of delays can sound good on vocals, but there's still nothing like a nice, warm chamber or plate reverb algorithm for wrapping around a voice.

Plan Ahead with Reverb and Panning

Although you can just move panpots around and add reverb until you're happy with the sound, try planning ahead by drawing a diagram of the intended soundstage (like the way theater people draw marks for where characters should stand). Place sounds farther back by lowering their level, and possibly adding more reverb and taking off some of the high frequencies. Bring sounds closer by making them louder, drier, and perhaps brighter. When mixing, a soundstage diagram can be a helpful guide to keep you on track.

Key Takeaways

- It's rare to hear recorded music where many tracks don't have at least some reverb.

- Algorithmic and convolution reverbs provide very different effects. Try both to determine which option best compliments your music.

- In most cases, you don't want a lot of low-frequency reverb with voice. Putting reverb on the vocal's higher frequencies is more common.

- Instruments with sustained notes like voice, organ, and strings can often benefit from low diffusion reverb settings. Too much diffusion may produce a "thick" reverb sound that competes with the main sound.

- High diffusion settings usually benefit percussive sounds.

Chapter 11

Using Mix Automation

Now that the mix is on its way, it's time to fine-tune levels and other parameters via *automation* that remembers your mixing moves.

After decades of engineers using analog mixing on consoles, automation came along and simplified the mixing process in unimagined ways. No longer would you blow a mix because you forgot to mute a bad note in the final chorus or introduce reverb during a key vocal phrase; now you would program the software to do the job for you.

With most modern DAWs, when you pull down a track's fader to reduce the level, track-based automation can store this move and repeat it every time you play that section of the song. When you set a track to read automation, on playback, any controls will move as if by magic (which if nothing else, looks pretty cool).

Furthermore, individual clips may have *clip automation* envelopes that are independent of the track automation. For example, clip automation could add a radical stuttering effect to a clip, while track automation could fade this out over a certain time.

Also note that signal processing and soft synth plug-ins have automatable parameters, although the specifics depend on the plug-in design. We'll cover this later.

What You Can Automate

For individual tracks, most programs can automate level, pan, mute, send level, and send pan, as well as track EQ parameters like gain, frequency, Q, filter type, etc. For bus tracks (if present), you typically can automate input gain, input pan, output pan, output volume, and bus EQ parameters.

MIDI tracks implement automation similarly, but have a different repertoire of controllable parameters. Volume, pan, mute, reverb, and chorus are common, but you can automate any parameter that responds to MIDI controllers by creating MIDI automation envelopes that transmit matching controller data.

Automation simplifies adding nuanced expressions to electronically oriented music. With automatable plug-ins, you can add variations that help the music come alive. Furthermore, you can overdub (and edit) automation data to tweak one parameter to perfection, then another, and so on.

Automation Basics

Most automation happens in one of four ways:

♦ Moving on-screen controls in real time and recording the motions.

♦ Creating or editing envelopes that change a parameter value over time.

♦ Recording data from an external hardware controller.

♦ Taking "snapshots" of control positions.

Recording automation moves is a different process compared to recording audio or MIDI data. With almost all programs you do not need (or want) the transport to be in record mode. This lets you record automation without being concerned about overwriting audio or MIDI data.

Different programs have different ways of arming (preparing) a parameter for automation, so consult your DAW's documentation for the details. One approach is right-clicking on a control and selecting a context menu option that specifies arming for automation (Fig. 11.1). Most tracks and plug-ins use somewhat standardized Write Automation and Read Automation operations (e.g., with VST plug-ins, click on a W button to write automation by varying the plug-in's controls, and an R button to read the automation). Both can be on at the same time, in which case new automation will overwrite previous automation data.

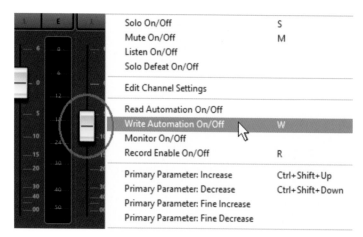

Figure 11.1 Right-click on a level fader in Cubase, then select Write Automation, and the program will begin storing your fader moves.

Most recording programs show your automation moves as an *envelope*—a line that displays the automation variations. Automation envelopes are usually either in their own lanes (these look like a subset of a track), superimposed on the track itself, or both (Fig. 11.2).

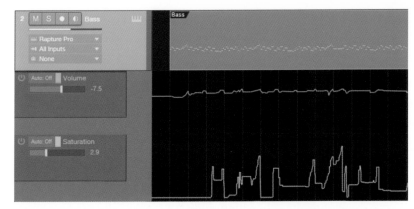

Figure 11.2 Studio One's automation lanes are controlling a bass track's volume as well as its saturation effect.

At a project's start, the automation envelope will be a straight line. The fader or other parameter being automated will set this base envelope level. Clicking on this line creates a *node* (a dot representing a specific value at a specific point on the timeline). You can drag this node higher or lower to change the automation value, and left or right to change the position where the automation change takes place. With enough nodes, you can draw very detailed automation moves. Also, you can often alter the shape of the line between nodes to create different curve types (Fig. 11.3).

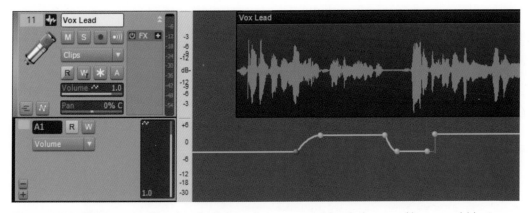

Figure 11.3 This automation data in Cakewalk has curved level changes (these could just as easily be straight lines). Toward the end, a "jump" change raises the level quickly.

Automation Methods

Let's go deeper into the four automation methods mentioned above.

Method 1: Record On-Screen Control Motion

This type of automation accommodates the human touch. You work intuitively by moving the fader as desired with your mouse (or your finger on a touch screen), but you can modify these moves later by editing the envelopes that these motions create. Although you can change only one parameter at a time with a mouse, with a hardware control surface (discussed later in this chapter) you can change multiple parameters simultaneously—like levels for the lead and background vocals.

The main way to create automation is similar for most programs. Enable automation recording and while holding down the mouse button, move a fader, panpot, or other parameter you want to automate. To stop writing automation, release the mouse button. Any existing automation data then resumes. You can punch in automation over existing automation. Some programs include a *latch* mode so that when you release the mouse button, the automation value persists instead of reverting to previous automation data.

To resume recording automation moves, click and hold the mouse button again. Because it's so simple to start and stop writing automation, you can "touch up" the automation easily if needed.

Method 2: Draw/Edit Envelopes

Moving an on-screen control while recording automation creates a corresponding automation envelope. You can edit an existing envelope or draw a new one from scratch, as well as show, hide, copy, paste, and perform other automation–related operations.

Because moving controls creates envelopes, and drawing envelopes moves the on-screen controls they affect, these methods are somewhat interchangeable. The method to use depends on what you need to do. For creating level changes, recording control motion works well. To sync changes to the beat, drawing envelopes will create more precise automation if you can snap envelope nodes to a rhythmic grid (see Fig. 11.4).

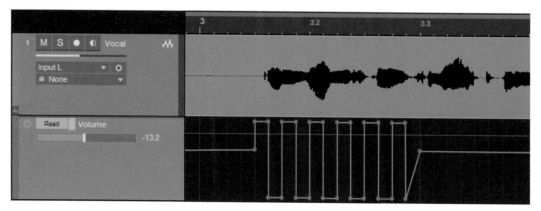

Figure 11.4 This envelope creates a stuttering effect by snapping drastic level changes to the rhythm.

In addition to creating nodes that specify automation envelope values, different programs will have ways to move, copy, delete, and paste nodes, and possibly shape the line between nodes. Consult your program's documentation.

Regarding automation of individual clips instead of tracks, you may be able to place nodes anywhere within the clip, or with simpler methods, have nodes only at the clip's start and end. Some programs (like

Pro Tools and Studio One) can change the clip gain, and the waveform graphic reflects these level changes. Ableton Live includes multiple clip editing options for both clip-specific parameters (Fig. 11.5) as well as standard mixer-oriented envelopes like level, pan, send, and crossfade assign.

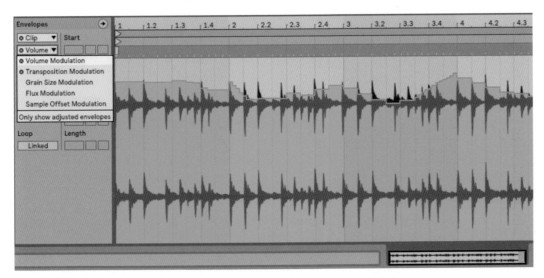

Figure 11.5 This clip envelope in Ableton Live controls volume modulation.

Method 3: Recording Automation Moves from External Control Hardware

Using an external hardware controller for automation follows the same basic procedure as recording a control's on-screen motion because the on-screen motion will be driven by the external hardware controller. After setting up a parameter to respond to an external control signal, you can record automation while moving the hardware controls. The automation data will appear as an envelope—just as if you'd moved an on-screen fader, pan control, or other parameter. Many hardware controllers feature motorized faders, allowing the faders to follow the envelope values on playback.

An external control surface with motorized faders (see Fig. 11.6) will likely include a feature called *touch faders*. With this feature, when you touch the fader, automation recording begins. When you let go of the fader, automation recording for that fader ends.

Hardware control surfaces are covered in more detail later in this chapter.

Figure 11.6 The PreSonus FaderPort 8 provides eight motorized faders as well as multiple switches. While designed to integrate tightly with the company's Studio One software, it can control parameters in other programs as well.

Method 4: Snapshot Automation

Snapshot automation is not a dynamic process; instead, it captures settings at a particular time as automation data. This is helpful for sudden changes rather than changes that fade in or out over time. For example, you might want lead guitar and drums to switch to a higher level when the guitar solo begins, then have both switch back to a lower level when the verse returns. You'd set the faders to the desired level at the beginning of the guitar solo, and take a snapshot of these settings. Those levels would remain in effect until you either take another snapshot, or start recording automation by some other method.

Automating Plug-Ins

One of automation's key strengths is in varying effects processing and synthesizer parameters for greater expressiveness. Static electronic sounds are sometimes not as sonically interesting as the ever-changing, complex nature of acoustic sounds. So using automation to change signal processing or virtual instrument parameters can add interest that increases a mix's effectiveness.

Different plug-ins offer different ways to record real-time automation moves. They use mostly the same options described above for automating mix parameters. However, the way you choose which parameter(s) you want to automate can vary considerably. What's more, not all soft synths work identically. Some can record control motion (called VST automation for VST plug-ins), while others respond only to automation via envelopes. Some accommodate both methods.

Fixed Controller Automation

This older approach assigns a parameter to a specific, unalterable MIDI controller number. If you automate using the plug-in's on-screen controls, then the controller number doesn't really matter. Tweak the control while recording automation, and the plug-in will play back those stored control gestures.

However, if you want to draw an envelope or use an external controller, you typically select the controller number from an automation menu that lists all automatable parameters. For example, if an instrument's volume responds to MIDI controller #7, then you would draw an envelope that generates controller #7, or program a hardware controller to generate controller #7, and record those messages. Either one of these options would record MIDI controller messages as envelopes that manipulate the volume on playback.

MIDI Learn

This is one of the best inventions ever for those who use hardware controllers. This feature lets you select a parameter you want to control, select the "MIDI Learn" option, and then move a control to complete the assignment process (Fig. 11.7). This gives you real-time control over the selected parameter using the knob, slider, or control wheel of your choice.

Figure 11.7 Right-clicking on the knob circled in red brings up the MIDI controller assignment menu for that parameter. It offers MIDI Forget as well as MIDI Learn so that it's easy to make and change assignments.

A plug-in's controls start off as unassigned. If you enable MIDI Learn for a control—typically done by selecting from a contextual menu (right-click or command-click)—you can vary a hardware control to tie the parameter to that control. This is very handy with MIDI keyboard controllers that include multiple faders, pads, rotary controls, and the like. Because MIDI Learn happens on a per-project basis, you needn't be overly concerned about consistent control assignments.

Using Hardware Control Surfaces

One of the problems with software-based recording and automation is that it lacks the hands-on, real-time control of traditional recording—drawing an envelope with a mouse is not the same as moving a fader, and some musicians crave tactile control. Although touchscreens provide an alternative to using a mouse, many people prefer physical hardware.

Hardware controllers aren't essential; you can use a mouse to draw envelopes or move on-screen faders. Drawing envelopes is often more precise than using faders. However, hardware control surfaces can help turn a mix into more of a performance, encourage spontaneity, and speed up your workflow when they include additional functionality (like transport controls).

Before describing how to install and use control surfaces, let's recap their history.

Traditional Mixing

Before digital audio appeared, all mixing surfaces had one control per function. Large-format analog consoles were expensive and huge, but having all controls at your fingertips made it easy to tweak anything you wanted in real time. Large-format digital consoles can use this approach as well. Prior to automation, mixdown often involved more than one person—in some cases because it was physically difficult for one person to reach all the mixer's controls (Fig. 11.8).

Figure 11.8 The Duality δelta Pro-Station from Solid State Logic has a layout that's representative of large-format mixing consoles.

Another important aspect to physical mixing was that real-time control invited "playing" the mixer, making it more of an instrument than just a way to balance levels. Many engineers would ride gain in time with the music, making subtle—or not so subtle—spontaneous adjustments to add character. When I did session work at Columbia Records, there was an engineer (with a lot of hits, by the way) who would slide the faders close to the right place, close his eyes, and move them subtly and rhythmically. I was impressed how this made the mix more lively, which was a lesson that stayed with me.

Also, moving faders and sends weren't the whole story. EQs had accessible knobs as well, which likewise invited real-time tweaking. The mixer was not a set-and-forget device, but in the hands of a talented engineer, it became a dynamic, living part of the music-making process. This type of thinking still exists in DJ and "groove" types of music, but overall, it seems mixing has become a more static process.

In the late 90s, Mackie and Digidesign created the HUI (Human User Interface) protocol for control surfaces. This established compatibility between hardware and computer-based recording programs. A few years later, the Mackie Control Universal established a more open protocol. Even today, most controllers (even those designed for specific programs) offer HUI or Mackie Control modes.

Current control surfaces range from touchscreens (Slate Media Raven series), to small, dedicated controllers for specific programs (Steinberg's CMC series of controllers for Cubase), to larger control surfaces like the Mackie MCU Pro or SSL Nucleus.

Control surfaces return some of the human element to mixing. Becoming familiar with a control surface's workflow can lead to a more fluid experience in the studio.

How to Choose a Control Surface

There are two main control surface families: general-purpose controllers designed to work with a wide range of software, and controllers dedicated to a specific program (which may also offer compatibility modes for other programs). Although a dedicated controller has the potential for a smoother user experience, if you use multiple programs, a dedicated controller may not be able to accommodate them. Make sure any controller not only supports your program of choice, but also the other software you use.

General-purpose controllers start with budget models that have, for example, 8 assignable MIDI knobs or faders. Programming these to control your software may be a tedious, manual affair, but accessory software for programming the device may exist to simplify matters.

Here are a few tips about control surfaces:

♦ If there's no built-in mapping to your program of choice, check whether your software has any presets or templates for general-purpose control surfaces that can get you started.

♦ You may not really need a controller if existing equipment can do the job. Some digital mixers include a MIDI fader layer that you can program to send controller information. Also, some keyboard controllers with faders or knobs include templates for controlling popular sequencing programs (Fig. 11.9). For relatively simple control surface applications that don't require motorized faders, these do the job.

Figure 11.9 Nektar's Impact LX88+, LX61+, and LX49+ keyboards can also function as control surfaces for Cakewalk by BandLab, Cubase, Digital Performer, FL Studio, GarageBand, Logic, Nuendo, REAPER, Reason, and Studio One.

♦ Controllers with motorized faders cost considerably more, but simplify mixing. An alternative, *nulling faders* are available on some devices. These don't move to reflect the current automation value but include indicators that show whether the fader is above or below an existing automation value. You can then set the fader's position to match the existing value before punching in to record additional fader moves.

♦ An expandable controller can provide flexibility to grow over time. An 8-channel moving fader setup may work for now, but then you'll want 16 channels, then 24... you know how *that* works. You should at least be able to bank-switch faders to different channel groups (e.g., 1-8, 9-16, etc.).

♦ There's more to control than fader levels. If possible, find a control surface that will let you tweak EQ settings, aux bus sends, etc.

♦ Check the footprint. A large, uncluttered control surface may be ideal ergonomically, but you may have to alter your studio setup to accommodate some of the larger models.

If possible, try before you buy. A control surface should be simple to use, feel good, and match well with your software. If you have good chemistry with a particular controller, you'll have a better studio experience.

Adding a Control Surface to Your Setup

The Mackie Control protocol is a *de facto* standard that handles most common mixing functions—faders, panpots, solos and mutes, transport controls, and the like. It may not cover aspects unique to a particular piece of software without additional programming. More specialized functions like opening and closing specific windows, editing plug-ins, setting preferences, etc. may be accessible from a control surface dedicated to a specific program.

Non-motorized faders are useful for controlling signal processing and soft synth parameters, but motorized faders are preferred for mixing. Because these follow automation moves and are touch-sensitive, you can leave the automation enabled, and the faders will follow along with whatever automation is already recorded on the track. The only drawback is the noise they make when moving, and some make a "clack" sound when they slam all the way off.

To add a specific control surface, check whether your software has an item under a menu like "Control Surfaces" (or the equivalent) for adding a specific control surface (Fig. 11.10).

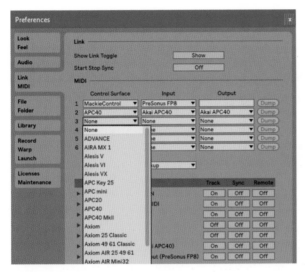

Figure 11.10 Ableton Live lists many hardware controllers. Choosing a controller sets up mapping between it and Ableton Live's parameters.

If your control surface isn't supported directly, set it to Mackie Control or HUI protocol if possible. There will probably be a template for at least one of them. If all else fails, you may have a "generic" template that you can use to custom-map some buttons or knobs to better match your software.

Automation Applications

Although adjusting levels while mixing is an important automation application, there are other ways automation can make better mixes—consider *attitude*. An orchestra's conductor doesn't just act like a metronome, but cajoles, leads, lags, and adds motion to the performance. A control surface can translate your human-generated gestures into machine-friendly automation.

Of course, the tracks will hopefully already include some degree of animation. But music seems to lose some of its impact in the recording process, and just as it's common to add a little EQ or harmonic enhancement, adding real-time changes to various aspects of a mix can create a more satisfying listening experience.

Adding Expressiveness with Controllers

Small, rhythmic level variations are often felt rather than heard. Although many musicians are satisfied to draw in level changes with a mouse, these can't have the same kind of spontaneity as changes that result from on-the-fly, creatively-inspired decisions over when tracks should dominate and when they should lay back further in the mix (Fig. 11.11).

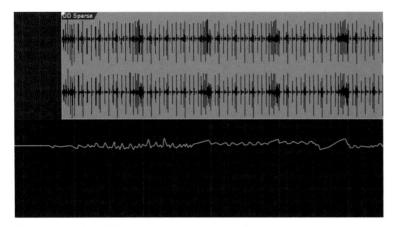

Figure 11.11 This track shows the result of using human-controlled fader automation to create rhythmic accents for a drum track. It would be time-consuming, and likely quite difficult to create this type of complex envelope by clicking and drawing.

At times you may encounter a situation where the automation moves are good, but the overall level needs to go up or down. There are three main fixes:

♦ **Select and move.** Select the nodes for the automation you want to change, then drag up or down. The Shift key is a somewhat standard modifier key to constrain movements to vertical changes.

♦ **Offset mode.** This mode typically changes fader functionality to not affect automation *per se,* but instead add an *offset* to the existing automation that increases or decreases all fader automation values proportionately. (This is sometimes referred to as *trim* automation.)

♦ **Adjust the channel input level.** This option varies the overall level going into the channel. However, it may affect track insert processors like distortion effects and dynamics processors, whose action is input–level dependent.

Aux Send Automation and Delays

To prevent delay from overwhelming a vocal track, insert the echo in an aux bus and bring up the send control selectively, to pick up just the end of phrases. When the phrase stops, the echoes from the last few words will continue—but before the vocals come back in, bring the aux send back down again to prevent echoes while the vocal is present. You'll probably want the send control assigned pre-fader.

Aux Sends and Reverb Splashes

I generally don't use huge reverberant spaces on mixes, but I will insert reverb with a long decay in one aux bus. If an isolated snare hit or held vocal note needs emphasis (or a dramatic pause calls for a reverb spillover), I'll turn up the aux send control long enough to send a signal spike into the reverb and create a tasty reverb splash.

Panning

When stereo was relatively new in the 60s, panning was popular as an effect ("Oh wow man, the guitars are flying across my head! *Pass the bong!*"). While going back to those gimmick-laden days is probably not a good idea, you should consider using subtle panning changes. For example, if you can pan a pad's left and right channels independently, panning both toward center sounds different compared to moving the panpots out to widen the stereo field. Also try expanding the sound incrementally so that as the pad continues, the stereo field widens.

Complementary Motion

Try this with bass and drums, or two instruments playing complementary rhythm parts. Vary their levels in opposing ways, but in time with the beat and very subtly—this should be felt rather than heard. Consider mixing the drums slightly louder for one measure with bass slightly back, and on the next measure, bump the bass up a bit and drop the drums correspondingly. The rhythmic variations build interest and can even give a somewhat hypnotic effect with dance-type music.

Mutes and Solos

Musicians have learned a lot from DJs (or at least, musicians with an open mind have)—and one popular technique is to solo a track for a break, or perhaps mute several tracks. Skilled remixers often create musical variations by playing multiple loops simultaneously, and then bringing them in and out (sometimes with level changes, sometimes with mute or solo) to build compositions. A tune might start with a looped pad, then fade in the kick, then the high hat, then the bass, and then have everything drop out except for the bass before bringing in some other melodic or rhythmic element.

As with the other examples mentioned thus far, you don't have to do this real time because you can program these changes as automation. But remember that mixing can be a performance—and sometimes inspiration can cause you to do fader moves and button presses in clever, non-repeatable ways. And when you do, you'll be happy that automation remembers those moves.

Mute vs. Change Level

Enabling a mute or solo causes a sudden, rapid level change that surprises the listener. Attempting the same type of change with faders will always sound somewhat different because the fader change will not be instantaneous. Thus, moving a fader from full off to full on—even if it's done fairly quickly—may cause a feeling of anticipation in the listener rather than surprise. Choose what's appropriate.

Plug-In Automation Applications

Automation can be about plug-ins as well as console parameters.

Better Chorusing and Flanging

I'm not a fan of the constant whoosh-whoosh-whoosh of LFO-driven chorus effects. Even when tempo-synched, the repetition can be more boring than AM radio (that's saying a lot). Fortunately, there are two simple workarounds:

♦ Use automation to vary the LFO rate control so that it changes constantly rather than locking into one tempo.

♦ Set the LFO to a very slow rate, or turn off LFO modulation, and automate an initial delay parameter (if possible—doing so may create clicks and pops). Play with the delay so the effect rises and falls in a musically appropriate way. Sometimes it's also worth overdubbing automation for feedback (regeneration) to add emphasis in certain parts.

Creative Distortion Crunch

A distortion plug-in's input level affects the distortion amount. To kick up the intensity without a major volume increase, turn up the plug-in's drive control or equivalent to add crunch. Assuming the signal is already clipping, turning it up more will create a more crunched sound, but being clipped, the output level won't increase by much. If it increases by too much, then automate the output as well to compensate.

If the distortion plug-in's drive parameter cannot be automated, automate the channel's trim parameter (the *input* level, not the fader-controlled *output* level) to change the level going to the distortion. If that doesn't provide a wide enough range, use the distortion as an aux bus effect, and then automate the effects send going to the bus to alter the distortion amount.

Emphasizing with EQ

Be careful when manipulating EQ in real time because even slight EQ boosts can have a major impact on the sound. But consider a situation where you want some big piano chords to become more prominent so they push the song more (for example in the final chorus). You could increase the level, but that may cause the piano to dominate, or lead to distortion. Another option is to automate a parametric stage's boost/cut control (use a fairly wide bandwidth in the 2 to 4 kHz range). When you want the piano to stand out, add a tiny bit of boost. Because the ear is most sensitive in this frequency range, even a small difference will give the piano more clarity. You could also boost in the low bass (below 150 to 200 Hz) to give the piano more power rather than more articulation.

Delay Feedback

This application sold me on effects automation. I often use synchronized echo effects on solos to heighten the intensity at the solo's peaks by increasing the delay feedback. This creates a "sea of echoes" effect. Sometimes this also involves bumping up the delay mix somewhat so there's more delay and less straight signal.

Using automation to bring up feedback, then reducing it before the effect becomes overbearing, can apply to any effect with a feedback parameter.

Sweeping the Parametric Wah

Automation is useful for wah effects because these changes can be more precise than moving a pedal with your foot. On one of my earliest sessions, the producer decided I should have recorded my guitar with a wah pedal. I was ready to re-record the part, but the engineer said he'd create the wah effect in the mix. He inserted a parametric, turned up the resonance, and swept the frequency control during the mixdown.

It sounded good, but not like a real wah. That's because a parametric has a flat response, with the peak poking above it. A real wah rejects frequencies around the resonant peak so you don't hear anything except the peak. However, it's possible to create a realistic wah effect with a parametric equalizer (Fig. 11.12).

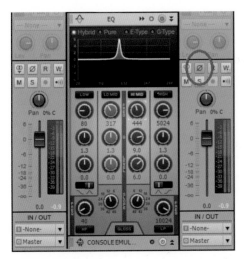

Figure 11.12 Two channels set up to create a wah effect. One channel is out of phase, which cancels all audio except the wah effect.

Here is the procedure to create a wah effect:

1.   Duplicate the track on which you want to add the wah effect.

2.   Invert the duplicate track's phase (polarity).

3. Begin playback; you won't hear anything because the two tracks will cancel each other out. You can verify this by changing one track's level slightly; you should now hear audio. Return to the original level when finished.

4. Turn on one band of bandpass EQ for the original track. Start with the controls as follows: Q = 3.3, Boost = 12 dB, Frequency = somewhere between 200 Hz and 1.5 kHz.

5. Assign the parametric filter frequency to automation, and sweep it from around 200 Hz to 1.5 kHz as desired.

Because of the high gain and narrow bandwidth, you'll need to watch out for distortion. You'll probably need to trim the controls carefully... but at least you won't have to spray the pedal potentiometer with contact cleaner.

Envelope-Based Tremolo

Nodes set at regular intervals can create the kind of periodic waveforms used with tremolo. It's difficult to draw a waveform like this freehand, but some programs provide a way to draw periodic waveforms (Fig. 11.13). If that's not possible, create a single instance of the desired waveform, then copy and paste it to make it longer. Tremolo circuits in old guitar amps used sine or triangle waves, but no law says you can't use sawtooth or irregular waves instead.

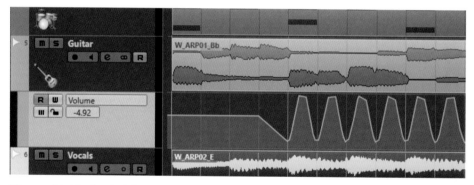

Figure 11.13 In Steinberg Cubase, you can draw a sine wave envelope (or envelopes using other periodic waveforms) that syncs to the grid. Here it's applied to guitar to produce a tremolo effect.

Pseudo Sample-and-Hold Effects

While we're in vintage-land, let's create synth-like sample-and-hold filter effects right out of the 1970s.

A sample-and-hold synth module samples a waveform at a slow, sub-audio rate, and creates a control signal equal to the sample's value. It uses this to control a parameter like a resonant filter's center frequency, and hold it for a particular duration (e.g., an eighth note). An eighth note later, it takes another sample, and then holds the filter at that new frequency. The effect creates a series of stepped filter changes—sort of like a quantized wah pedal. The Parametric Wah setup described previously produces a classic resonant filter effect.

Creating a sample-and-hold, stepped-type automation control signal requires drawing an envelope because you can't move a control fast enough to create instant filter frequency changes. Fortunately, you can usually provide an instant transition from one automation node to another where both snap to the grid. As mentioned above, some programs allow for drawing waveforms; if available, a stepped, random waveform is perfect for this application.

Virtual Instrument Automation Applications

Automation can make virtual instruments more versatile.

Virtual Guitar Feedback

I love the sound of a guitar going into feedback when it kicks up an octave and a fifth (19 semitones) higher, two octaves higher, or two octaves and a fifth (31 semitones) higher. You can create a similar effect with a soft synth or sampler.

Create your basic patch around one oscillator, tune another oscillator (typically a sine wave) to the feedback frequency, then automate its level. As a note starts to decay, fade up the level of the oscillator creating feedback, like how a guitar generates a sympathetic tone when it starts feeding back. Add some mod wheel vibrato, or manipulate the pitch bend wheel, to animate the sound further.

Suboctave with Bass

A similar trick works for bass sounds, but in this case, you want to tune the second oscillator an octave lower so that turning up its level brings in a big, fat suboctave. In this application, try using a sawtooth or pulse wave with some low-pass filtering for the sub-harmonic. I've also done the reverse in breaks—when the bass keeps going and the drums drop out, pull back on the suboctave. Then, when the drums come back in again, push the suboctave and it will sound really big.

Synthesizer Pads

Pads and other big-sounding patches often use chorusing. Try automating the chorus modulation frequency (and feedback control, if available), slowly making adjustments so that the pad is constantly changing and evolving.

Fun with Ostinato and Arpeggiation

For rhythmic synth tracks (e.g., arpeggios or ostinato phrasing), three of my favorite parameters for automation are filter cutoff, filter envelope decay, and amplitude envelope decay. Changing these in real time can make what might be an overly repetitive part far more interesting. When mixing, also try tweaking the control that ties velocity to filter cutoff (if the filter cutoff wasn't varied in the original recording) to emphasize the dynamics.

Key Takeaways

♦ You can create automation data in multiple ways—moving an on-screen control, using a control surface, drawing envelopes, and taking "snapshots" of control positions.

♦ You can automate plug-in as well as mixer parameters.

♦ MIDI Learn makes it easy to map hardware controls to software parameters.

♦ Hardware control surfaces can help you regain some of the hands-on feel of traditional consoles.

♦ Automation can add expressiveness to plug-ins and virtual instruments by creating interesting variations.

♦ Bringing aux send effects in and out with automation makes sure they don't overstay their welcome.

Chapter 12

Review and Export

You've cleaned up the tracks, added processing, controlled the dynamics, set a great balance among all your tracks, and used automation to tweak levels and other parameters. This is your last chance to make any final changes before the mastering process.

Remember that as with so many aspects of life, less is more. Live with the mix for a while and critique what you hear. Be as brutal as possible.

- Does the beginning pull someone in like a tractor beam?

- Do parts compete with each other, reducing their effectiveness?

- If the focus is the vocal, do all the other instruments sharpen that focus when the singer is singing?

- Does *every single song element,* from the notes themselves to the signal processing, serve the song and enhance the message it's trying to convey?

- Is there some needed but missing element, like an extra hand-percussion part toward the end to maintain interest?

- If you mute a track, do you miss it—or does muting it allow the other tracks to shine?

- Are you mixing creatively by selectively dropping out or bringing in tracks as appropriate? This type of mixing is the foundation for a lot of dance music.

- Is there enough cowbell? (Kidding!)

Mastering While Mixing—Pros and Cons

Let's address a controversial topic before proceeding: mastering while mixing. When tape ruled, mastering was a separate process from mixing for several reasons:

- Albums (collections of songs) were popular. A mastering engineer transformed all the disparate mixes into a cohesive listening experience with similar dynamics and tonal qualities. With today's software, it's easy to load up projects consecutively and evaluate them for consistency. With traditional recording, that was extremely difficult—especially before automation became commonplace.

♦ The mastering engineer also worked with the producer and artist to determine the best song sequence. With vinyl, this was not always an artistic decision. For example, a record's inner grooves were more prone to distortion, so softer songs were often the last song on a side. Also, the album sides needed to be of approximately equal length.

♦ Tradeoffs were required for different delivery media. With vinyl, too much bass could cause needles to jump out of grooves on playback. Creating a good master was a matter of both experience and trial and error.

Mastering engineers commonly generated multiple test pressings before finding the right balance of level, length, frequency response, etc.

♦ There would sometimes be last-minute tweaks made in mastering, like speeding up the master tape a few percent to give it a brighter, tighter sound. This was not possible to do while mixing unless the multitrack recorder had variable speed.

♦ Mastering suites were only required to work on two tracks at a time, so facilities could buy the finest gear possible—the kind of gear you couldn't afford if you needed several units to process tracks from a multitrack tape recorder.

♦ Mixing and mastering were considered specialized skills. A great mix engineer was not necessarily a great mastering engineer, and vice-versa.

With digital audio, most of the technical constraints for mastering are gone. Although this simplifies the mastering process, it's still valid to think of mixing and mastering as separate skills.

With so many musicians today doing everything themselves—recording, playing, engineering, producing, mixing, and yes, even mastering—it's important to have an objective set of ears for a final project review. If that's you, great. If not... you need a mastering engineer.

Online and Automated Mastering Services

You may be wondering whether online and automated mastering services can do the job for you. The answer is yes and no. If you want to post a live recording of your band online as a souvenir for your fans, you might not be able to justify a pro mastering engineer's expense. I've always defined mastering as "making what comes out sound better than what went in," and automated mastering using algorithms can achieve that in some situations (Fig. 12.1).

Figure 12.1 Although the Lurssen Mastering Console program from IK Multimedia can't do "waveform surgery" like cutting song sections or noise reduction, it can give excellent results.

For a mission-critical project upon which your career depends, a good mastering engineer will make decisions no machine could make—like shortening your mix to remove an overindulgent guitar solo without anyone ever noticing, bringing up the level somewhat on a fill, or applying restoration software to minimize residual hiss.

Mastering While Mixing

Mastering adds any needed dynamics, EQ, or other processing to your mix. So it seems logical that you could, at least in theory, add these processors to your master bus and accomplish the same result. While that's possible, I still prefer treating mixing and mastering as separate processes, particularly for album assembly and song sequencing. I'll take the mixes and load them into Studio One's Project page, which lets you load individual tracks, sequence them in any order, set the timing between songs, add overall processing to all tracks or just some tracks, insert markers to indicate song beginnings, and set fades. Being able to hear all the tracks in this context makes it easier to decide if each track works as part of a complete, integrated whole.

Even if you record only singles, to ensure consistency, it's worth mastering them as if they were on an album. If someone assembles a playlist of your greatest hits, you don't want them to experience level and tonal swings while they listen.

Prepping Files for a Mastering Engineer

If you decide to use a mastering engineer, consider the following best practices before you export any files:

◆ Leave headroom. Your peaks shouldn't hit higher than –6 dB; –10 dB is probably better.

◆ Don't insert any processors in the master bus, especially maximizers or compressors. Doing so will limit what mastering engineers can do. And keep in mind that they have the best tools.

- Be clear about what you want. I've often said there are at least 20 valid ways to master a piece of music, but the only one that matters is the one that fulfills the artist's vision. It's helpful to give the engineer examples of music whose *sound* you like (even if you're not a fan of the music itself).

- Don't add fade-outs or fade-ins unless they're unusual. Let the mastering engineer do an appropriate fade based on your input.

Whether you master inside the program or give a file to a mastering engineer, eventually you'll need to export your song to a final stereo mix.

Export Your Mixed File

Exporting your song is the easiest and most universal way to create a final stereo mix. You adjust all the settings exactly as you want (EQ, levels, etc.), including any automation that's in play. When the mix is perfect, you can choose an export option (typically from a file menu) and render the file in any one of several formats, sample rates, and bit resolutions.

Main File Types

When exporting, you will choose between three main families of file types:

- **Compressed audio.** *Compressed* audio doesn't refer to dynamic range compression (as described in Chapter 8), but *data* compression that reduces the file size. Data-compressed files take up less storage in portable players, stream more quickly over the web, and take less time to send via email. The maximum size reduction occurs with *lossy* formats, like MP3, AAC (Apple), Ogg Vorbis, and WMA (Windows). To save space, these formats remove audio data judged to be inaudible. Technically, this is more a process of data *omission* than data compression. You can choose how much data to remove—the tradeoff is lower-quality sound for smaller file sizes.

- **Lossless compressed audio.** This format is more like a .zip file—de-compressing the file restores the original file, so there's no lost data. The most popular format is FLAC (Free Lossless Audio Codec); it's the preferred lossless file format in Windows 10. Apple's alternative is Apple Lossless. Compared to compressed audio, the tradeoff for greater fidelity is larger file sizes.

- **Uncompressed audio.** The main formats are WAV (Windows) and AIFF or AIF (Apple). These are preferred by mastering engineers and CD duplication houses.

Lossy formats are becoming less popular as bandwidth increases and memory becomes cheaper, but most programs allow exporting in a variety of formats (Fig. 12.2).

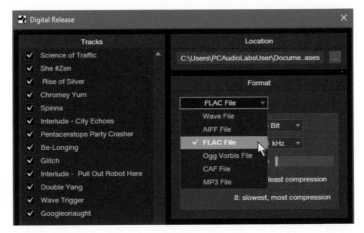

Figure 12.2 Studio One's Project Page can export a collection of songs or an album in a variety of digital formats (these are from the album *Trigger,* by Bryan Ferry guitarist Quist).

Sample Rates and Bit Depth

In addition to choosing the export format, you need to decide on a sample rate and bit depth (i.e., audio resolution). We touched on this previously, but we didn't go into much depth because by the time you reach the mixing stage, the sample rate and bit depth has already been set.

When exporting, however, you have the opportunity to choose from a variety of formats.

Tech Talk: Sample Rates and Resolution

Analog-to-digital conversion translates audio from microphones, pickups, and instruments—all of which provide varying voltages—into computer data. More accurate conversion means higher audio quality. Because a computer can't understand a changing voltage unless it's presented as a series of numbers, an *analog-to-digital converter* (ADC) is used to measure the incoming analog voltage thousands of times a second and convert each measurement into computer–friendly digital data (binary numbers). The number of measurements the converter takes each second is the *sample rate*, also called *sampling frequency. Bit resolution* refers to the accuracy with which the ADC measures the incoming audio signal. More bits means higher resolution.

Here are the most popular sample rate and bit depth choices for uncompressed files:

♦ 44.1 kHz with 16-bit resolution is the standard for CDs.

♦ 96 kHz with 24-bit resolution is the standard for high-resolution audio and some DVDs, although some audiophiles prefer 192 kHz (or even 384 kHz) with 24 bits of resolution. It remains to be seen whether high-resolution will get commercial traction.

For compressed files, the primary specification is how many kilobits of data can stream in one second (abbreviated kbps). Here are some popular bit rate choices for streaming audio:

♦ 128 kbps is the lowest common denominator for streaming audio. It saves space, but there's an obvious lack of sound quality.

♦ 256 kbps provides reasonably good fidelity.

♦ 320 kbps is the highest MP3 rate. At this rate, the typical consumer won't hear any significant difference compared to CD quality.

♦ Higher bit rates, like 384 kbps, are available for compressed formats other than MP3.

Bouncing Mixes Inside the Project

Today's music software allows non-traditional options for mixing down your project to a finished file. One of these is bouncing down all of a project's tracks to a new track within the same project. Your program will likely have a bounce option where you select the tracks you want to bounce (usually all of them), and then specify the mix's destination track. The bouncing often occurs from the master bus, so make sure the level doesn't go above 0 dBFS.

This approach allows creating several different mixes, each saved in its own track. You can then compare the various mixes to decide which one you like, and export the best one. Most programs have an exclusive solo option, which means that soloing a track automatically mutes all other tracks. This makes it easy to do A/B comparisons among tracks (Fig. 12.3).

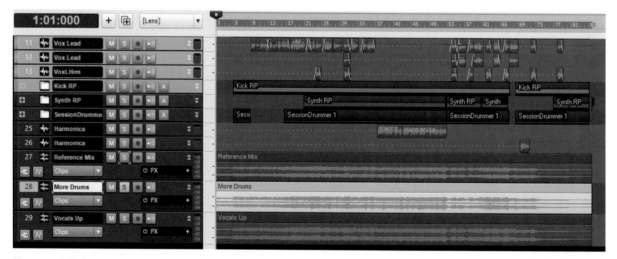

Figure 12.3 Tracks 27, 28, and 29 are internal bounces from the project's tracks. Each is a variation on the mix.

Another advantage of bouncing multiple mixes within a project is that you can choose parts of different tracks and splice them together into your final mix. For example, you might have nailed everything except the chorus in one mix, but the chorus was perfect in a different mix. In this case, you can cut the preferred chorus, substitute it for the one you don't like, and then export the final mix.

A final advantage of creating mixes within a project is that when you save the project, you also save the mixes. This is helpful for those who do their mastering "inside the box" and want an easy way to archive their mixes.

Check Your Mix Over Different Systems

Before you sign off on a mix, check it over a variety of systems. If the mix sounds good under all different conditions, your job is done.

A home studio allows the luxury of leaving a mix and coming back to it the next day when you're fresh, and also after you've had a chance to listen over several different systems to decide if you want to make any tweaks. This is one reason why automation is wonderful—if everything is perfect about a mix except one little thing that bothers you, you can edit the automation to fix that problem.

I can't emphasize enough the importance of mixing until you're satisfied. There's nothing worse than hearing one of your tunes six months later and kicking yourself because of some flaw you didn't take the time to correct, or some issue you didn't notice because you were in too much of a hurry to complete the mix.

However, be equally careful not to beat a mix to death. Quincy Jones once told me he felt that recording with synthesizers and sequencing was like "painting a 747 with Q-Tips." A mix is a performance, and if you overdo it, you'll lose the spontaneity that can add excitement. A mix that isn't perfect but conveys passion will always be more fun for listeners than one that's perfect to the point of sterility. As insurance, don't always re-record over your mixes—when you listen back to them the next day, you might find that an earlier mix was the one that sounded most alive.

In fact, you may not even be able to tell too much difference among all the mixes anyway. A record producer once told me about mixing literally dozens of takes of the same song because he kept hearing small issues and making changes that seemed really important at the time. In the middle of the process, he had to go away for a few weeks. When he returned to review the mixes, he couldn't tell any difference among almost all of the versions. Be careful not to waste time making changes that no one, not even you, will care about.

One last tip: once you've captured your ultimate mix, create a couple extra versions, such as an instrumental-only mix, a mix without the solo instrument, or one with the vocals mixed higher. These additional mixes can come in handy if you need to re-use your music for a film or video score, or create extended dance mixes. Be prepared!

Key Takeaways

♦ You've reached the last part of the music creation process, so this is your last chance to make any changes.

♦ There are both pros and cons to mastering while mixing.

♦ Automated mastering algorithms can sometimes be all you need, but there's much to be said for handing off your mix to a professional mastering engineer.

♦ When exporting your mix for a mastering engineer, make sure it's prepared properly.

♦ Lossy data compression reduces file size, but degrades fidelity. Lossless data compression, like FLAC files, doesn't reduce file size as much but retains fidelity.

♦ Mastering engineers prefer uncompressed audio (WAV and AIF files).

♦ Export your mix at 44.1 kHz with uncompressed audio if it will end up on CD. For lossy formats, choose the appropriate tradeoff of file size versus fidelity.

♦ Bouncing mixes within a project to create multiple stereo mixes can offer several advantages.

♦ Always check a mix over different systems before signing off on it.

Appendix

Mixing with Noise

I've placed this subject in an appendix because if you've made it this far, you've probably found some value in what I've written and won't dismiss this out of hand as you dissolve in gales of laughter. But most people who've been brave enough to try this technique swear that it really does work… see what you think.

Why Mixing Can Be Challenging

A mix doesn't compare levels to an absolute standard; all the tracks are interrelated. As an obvious example, the lead instruments usually have higher levels than the rhythm instruments. But there are much smaller hierarchies. Suppose you have a string pad part, and the same part delayed a bit to produce chorusing. To avoid having excessive peaking when the signals reach maximum amplitude at the same time, as well as better preserve any rhythmic "groove," you'll probably mix the delayed track around 6 dB behind the non-delayed track.

Top mixing engineers are in such demand because they've trained their ears to discriminate among tiny level and frequency response differences. They're basically juggling the levels of multiple tracks, making sure that each one occupies its proper level with respect to the other tracks. The more tracks involved in a miz, the more intricate this juggling act becomes.

However, there are certain essential elements of any mix—some instruments that just *have* to be prominent and mixed fairly closely in level to one another because of their importance. Ensuring that these elements are clearly audible and perfectly balanced is crucial to creating a mix that sounds good over a variety of systems. Perhaps the lovely high end of some bell won't translate on a cheap boombox, but if the average listener can make out the vocals, leads, the beat, and the bass, you have the high points covered.

Our ears are less sensitive to changes in relatively loud levels than in relatively soft ones. This is why many veteran mixers initially work on a mix at low levels. At low volume, it is easier to tell if the important instruments are out of balance with respect to each other. At higher levels, balance differences become harder to detect.

The Backstory Behind Using Noise

Like many other techniques that ultimately turn out to be useful, I discovered this one by accident. Once when working in a studio in Florida, I noticed that mixes I'd done with the air conditioner on often sounded better than the ones I'd completed when it was off. That got me thinking about the common practice of "playing the music in the car" as the final test of whether a mix is going to work or not. In both cases, the background noise masks low-level signals, making it easier to focus on the signals that make it above the noise.

Curious whether this phenomenon could be defined more precisely, I started injecting pink noise into the console while mixing. As it turns out, mixing with a pink noise source as one of the channels (panned to center) is a great way to check whether a song's crucial elements are mixed with equal emphasis. This just about forces you to listen at relatively low levels, because the noise is really obnoxious—but more importantly, the noise adds a sort of "cloud cover" over the music. And just as mountain tops poke out of a cloud cover, so here the sonic peaks emerge out of the noise.

Mixing with Noise

When using this technique, you'll want to add in the pink noise *very* sporadically during a mix because the noise covers up high frequency sounds like hi-hat. You cannot get an accurate idea of the complete mix while you're mixing with noise injected into the mixer. What you *can* do is make sure that all the important instruments are being heard properly.

Getting Started with Noise Injection

Typically, I'll take a mix to the point where I'm fairly satisfied with the sound. Then I'll add in lots of pink noise—no less than 10 dB below 0 with dance mixes, for example, which typically have restricted dynamics anyway—and start analyzing.

While listening through the song, I pay special attention to vocals, snare, kick, bass, and leads (with this much noise, you're not going to hear much else in the song anyway). It's very easy to adjust their relative levels, because there's a limited range between overload at higher levels and dropping below the noise at lower levels. If all the crucial sounds make it into that "window" and can be heard clearly above the noise without distorting, you have a head start toward an equal balance.

Setting Levels with Noise

Note that the noise test can also uncover level problems. If you can hear a hi-hat or other minor part fairly high above the noise, it's probably too loud.

I'll generally run through the song a few more times, carefully tweaking each track for the right relative balance. Then it's time to take out the noise. First, it's an incredible relief not to hear that annoying hiss! Second, and more importantly, you can now get to work balancing the supporting instruments so that they work well with the lead sounds you've tweaked.

Noise Zones

Although so far I've only mentioned instruments being above the noise floor, there are actually three distinct zones created by the noise: a low-level zone containing sounds that are totally masked by the noise (inaudible), a high-level zone containing sounds above the noise (clearly audible), and a "melded" zone, containing instruments that aren't loud enough to stand out or soft enough to be masked, so they blend in with the noise. I find that mixing rhythm parts to sound melded can be quite effective, providing the noise is adjusted to a level suitable for the rhythm parts.

Summary

Overall, I spend very little mixing time using the injected noise. But often, it's the factor responsible for making the mix sound good over multiple systems.

Mixing with noise may sound crazy, but don't knock it until you give it a try. With a little practice, you'll find ways to make noise work for you.

About the Author

Musician/author Craig Anderton is an internationally recognized authority on music and technology. His onstage career spans from the 60s with the group Mandrake, through the early 2000s with electronic groups Air Liquide and Rei$$dorf Force, to the "power duo" EV2 with Public Enemy's Brian Hardgroove, and EDM-oriented solo performances.

He has played on, produced, or mastered over 20 major label recordings, did pop music session work in New York in the 1970s on guitar and keyboards, played Carnegie Hall, and more recently, has mastered well over a hundred tracks for various artists.

In the mid-80s, Craig co-founded *Electronic Musician* magazine. As an author, he's written over 26 books on musical electronics and over a thousand articles for magazines like *Keyboard, Sound on Sound, Rolling Stone, Pro Sound News, Guitar Player, Mix,* and several European publications.

Craig has lectured on technology and the arts (in 10 countries, 38 U.S. states, and three languages), and done sound design work for companies like Alesis, Gibson, Peavey, PreSonus, Roland, and Steinberg.

Please check out some of his music at youtube.com/thecraiganderton, visit his web site at craiganderton.com, and follow him on twitter @craig_anderton.